APPLAUDIENCE

Born to Sing! The Autobiography of Dale Lind
Cantor, Entertainer & Entrepreneur

*To Allen,
He keeps our soles
in good shape!
In friendship,
Dale Lind.*

Order this book online at www.trafford.com/07-3070
or email orders@trafford.com

Most Trafford titles are also available at major online book retailers.

© Copyright 2008 Dale I. Lind.

All rights reserved. No part of this publication may be reproduced, stored in a retrieval system, or transmitted, in any form or by any means, electronic, mechanical, photocopying, recording, or otherwise, without the written prior permission of the author.

Note for Librarians: A cataloguing record for this book is available from Library and Archives Canada at www.collectionscanada.ca/amicus/index-e.html

Printed in Victoria, BC, Canada.

ISBN: 978-1-4251-6626-7

We at Trafford believe that it is the responsibility of us all, as both individuals and corporations, to make choices that are environmentally and socially sound. You, in turn, are supporting this responsible conduct each time you purchase a Trafford book, or make use of our publishing services. To find out how you are helping, please visit www.trafford.com/responsiblepublishing.html

Our mission is to efficiently provide the world's finest, most comprehensive book publishing service, enabling every author to experience success. To find out how to publish your book, your way, and have it available worldwide, visit us online at www.trafford.com/10510

 www.trafford.com

North America & international
toll-free: 1 888 232 4444 (USA & Canada)
phone: 250 383 6864 ♦ fax: 250 383 6804 ♦ email: info@trafford.com

The United Kingdom & Europe
phone: +44 (0)1865 722 113 ♦ local rate: 0845 230 9601
facsimile: +44 (0)1865 722 868 ♦ email: info.uk@trafford.com

10 9 8 7 6 5 4 3 2

Dedication

I dedicate this book to my
beloved wife Jessie, whose love and
devotion I will always cherish.
She made our life together magical,
and will always be the
keeper of my heart.

Applaudience: The Autobiography of Dale Lind

TABLE OF CONTENTS

Prologue i
Overture iii
Tenement Life 1
In The Beginning 7
My Cup Runneth Over–in My Father's House 11
Born To Sing 17
My *Bar-Mitzvah* Day 23
The Crash Of '29 27
Greener Pastures 29
The Congress Theatre Caper .35
A Century Of Progress (the World's Fair) 39
New Horizons 41
Strange Happenings 45
A Miracle 53
Chicago's High-hat Club: Our Debut 57
"Sing & Swing Unlimited" 61
Chicago's West Side 65
An Act Of Fate 69
Show Time In The Army 73
War Experiences 79
A Near Death Experience 85
Who Shall Live And Who Shall Die 91
The Invasion 97
Kaye & Durocher 103
Command Performance 107
Homeward Bound 113
Home At Last—Free Again 117
The Schvitzbud (sweatbath) .119
Climbing The Ladder 123

Table of Contents

Star Billing In Vegas, A Fantasy Fulfilled 127
Reunions & A Newcomer 135
Ups & Downs In Paradise 141
Strange Destiny 147
The Birth Of Israel 155
Who Said It Is Better To Venture & Lose? 159
My Kids—The Troupers 163
Fulfillment—And Grief 169
An Act Of God—The Sting Of Fate 177
The Show Must Go On 183
Overcoming Adversity 187
Eulogy For My Father 193
Lifting Myself Up 197
And The Young Shall Lead Us 201
Returning To My Spiritual Calling 205
Parties & Cruise Ships 213
A Harrowing Experience 219
The Holy Land Of Our Ancestors 223
A New Generation 231
Stunning Family Memories .235
A Heart-rending Reunion 243
Atonement 245
Retirement 249
Giving Back 251
Thoughts & Observations 255
My Ideology 259
Epilogue 263
About the Author 265

Prologue

I am most fortunate that my restless spirit forced me to delve into so many different facets of life. Becoming a cantorial prodigy at the mere age of nine, matured me much more than my peers. By the time I became *Bar-Mitzvah* (a coming-of-age religious ceremony performed at age thirteen), I didn't need to be lectured to by my elders about coming into adulthood. I was already a young adult when I was cantoring and leading my people in prayer.

Traveling as a prodigy throughout the United States and Canada, and being surrounded by adults for most of my life, I formed different perspectives than other children my age. Attending Hebrew school and later a *Yeshiva* (Jewish school for higher learning), I learned the ethics and values of my forefathers. That, and the love of my family, fulfilled my spiritual needs as I was growing up. God had blessed me with a powerful singing voice, and studying with operatic coaches and language teachers, I became well-versed in drama and play acting. Facing an audience was as natural for me as swimming is for a duck. Later, as my profession changed from the serious goal of opera, I began entertaining audiences by presenting a variety of songs in many languages. That made singing a lot more fun as I developed a closer relationship with my audiences.

My brothers and I were extremely lucky, being blessed with great voices. Harmonizing as we did from the time we were youngsters gave us the impetus and determination to escape the "tenement'" mentality of New York's East Side. We literally sang our way out of the ghetto.

After years of traveling with our dad as a cantorial group, our family settled down in Chicago. My brothers and I began working as an American trio and overcame the label of being called "a Jewish act." With dogged determination we finally succeeded as "The Three Lind Brothers" and performed in all the different show business venues. Entertaining side by side with some of the greatest stars of stage, screen and radio, and through World War II as GI's, we were catapulted into headliners from Vegas to Broadway.

After years of performing together, our trio separated in the middle 1960's. I returned to my life as a clergyman and reveled in my duties. My different vocations gave me the rare opportunity to chant, sermonize, entertain and philosophize. They also afforded me the knowledge and insight into what makes people tick, and what we're all about. As a result, I have been able to express my ideology of life in these pages, as I experienced it for more than fourscore years.

It is a rare privilege for me to transfer my story to the pages of a book. I am most grateful for that opportunity, and hope I will be able to bring a modicum of pleasure and profound thoughts to my readers.

OVERTURE

My gratitude goes to my loved ones and the many friends who have graced my life. I would especially like to thank, first and foremost, my beloved parents, Eva (Chave) and Joshua (Yehoshua), to whom I owe so much. They nurtured and taught me right from wrong. Through them I learned about caring and compassion for others regardless of race, creed, or color. Not only did my parents teach me about life's true values, but I also learned through their example about moral integrity and dedication to man's highest ideals. Finally, they provided all of our family with the kind of home that was filled with good humor and love, and they inspired us with an extraordinary appreciation of music that became the central force of our lives. I shall respect and treasure my parents as long as I live.

To my darling wife Jessie, my soul-mate for over sixty years, goes the largest part of my love—deep down to the very core of my being. Jessie has been my rock of courage, strength, and devotion in all that we have shared together. I can't imagine what my life, with all of its ups and downs, would have been without her. I shall always love, honor, and cherish her.

Kudos to our talented children, Cary and Barbara, and Cary's lovely wife Sandy. They have always been there for us when we needed them musically, and in all our endeavors. My special thanks and gratitude go to Cary for his exceptional piano accompaniment and for his splendid conducting of my choir.

As of this writing, my right and left arms have left me. Losing my brother Murray some years ago, and my brother Phil more recently, has been a devastating blow to me and all the family. It seems like only yesterday when my brothers and I were like the Three Musketeers with their famous motto, "All for one—and one for all." As I reminisce about all the audiences we faced together, I can only pray that wherever my brothers Murray and Phil are, as they read about our life and times together, they are *kvelling*—beaming with pride. From our original five siblings, we are now two, having recently lost our sister Norma to Alzheimer's. My sister, Selma and I, now find great comfort in each other and in reminiscing about the wonderful days and years we enjoyed together, as all five of us laughed and sang constantly through good times and bad.

A special tribute and my deep appreciation go to my gifted and loving daughter Barbara. It was she who coined the phrase and title of this book. At age 4-1/2, performing her first show with Cary and me, she was asked by a member of the audience what she liked best about her performance. Barb replied, "I loved the *Applaudience!*"

I also wish to thank my granddaughters, Joanna and Allison, for typing, Barbara and my daughter-in-law, Sandy, for editing, and my niece, Mary Beth Crum, for publishing advice and assistance.

My heartfelt thanks go to my editor and friend, author Dr. Gwendoline Y. Fortune, for her keen insight and professional advice.

Finally my sincere thanks goes to Lee Roesner and Brian McGowan of Paradigm Graphic Design who's creativity added so much to my book.

Chapter 1

TENEMENT LIFE

I was all of five years old when we moved from Brooklyn to 173 Henry Street, on the East Side of New York. We lived on the seventh floor of a tenement building because there was no eighth! With no elevator in the building, the higher you went, the less rent you paid. Our sainted mother was always *shlepping* groceries and things for us up and down the stairs. I remember Dad would say,

"Chave, let me carry the bags."

And Mom would answer, "Shiye, you want to get a *kille* (rupture)? You have to sing tomorrow in the *shul* (synagogue)."

Dad would kid her with, "So what if I sing in my synagogue with a *kille*, will they fire me?"

My Dad used to say his job was easier than the other cantors because every time the "El" train went by during services, he could skip a few pages.

To be a kid on the East Side in the twenties was a great experience. Life was so much simpler then. We played "Stickball" and "Kick the Can" in the streets, and everybody had a nickname. I was such a lousy athlete that when I got up to bat, all the kids would yell, "Nobody's Up!" And most of the time they were right, because I rarely hit the elusive ball. Still, they kept me on the team because I fielded well.

Knowing how badly I felt when they yelled, "Nobody's Up," my dad kept assuring me that someday I would be somebody special. When he started training me as a boy-cantor, I was only seven years old. But he recognized an innate talent as he proclaimed, "Dovidel, you're going to be a wonder boy-cantor." In a way, this would be a great fulfillment for my dad as well.

As a youngster in Lemberg, Galicia, where he was born, the famous European cantor, Zaydel Rovner, took my father under his wing as an apprentice. Dad's parents were deeply thrilled that such a famous man would even consider their son good enough to teach and travel throughout Europe with him. Rovner taught him the basics of music and the traditional melodies of our people. Years later, however, Dad taught himself how to compose and arrange choral music without anyone else's help. The talent was always there deep down in his soul. He just needed time for it to emerge. And emerge it did! Many years later he had won the admiration of his colleagues, students, and the Jewish musical world for his genius in the liturgy and magnificent choral works.

As my father traveled with Cantor Rovner through Bucovina, Rumania, fate intervened. A matchmaker did her magic and brought him together with my mother, Eva Sonenschein, who came from a most prodigious family. In no time at all, barely knowing each other they were married. Forget any thought of romance or as the song says, "Getting to Know You." It was "a given" that they would learn to love each other. It has always been amazing to me how most of those marriages lasted a lifetime—even more so than marriages following long courtships and based on familiarity, passion, romance and other considerations.

Eventually, my parents made their way to the USA, which foreigners called "The Golden Land." This was after all America—the Land of Freedom, Justice and Opportunity. This was the country where great things could be accomplished. And so they were—by many who had the ambition and energy, with a little bit of luck thrown in, which we call *mazel!* Having come from Europe, my folks always felt extremely fortunate to be here in America, where streets were supposedly paved in gold.

I was eight years old when I began learning intricate coloratura passages, progressing rapidly because it was like a game to me. I delighted in matching phrases with adult cantors who were students of my dad. Some of them did not have enough agility in their voices for coloratura phrases and were amazed that I could do what they could not. They kept repeating to my father, "*Dovid* is growing into a cantor!"

My dad agreed, saying, "Dovid will become the youngest cantor in history."

I studied day and night with Dad, learning to sight-read music. Everything he wrote for me, I gobbled up so quickly that my dad was absolutely stunned. I mastered breath control and learned to sing a *cappela* (without accompaniment), which was the only acceptable way in orthodox synagogues. My only musical instrument was a tuning fork or pitch pipe used to set the key. Dad also taught me to pronounce the Hebrew with an Eastern European Jewish accent.

Even though I was missing out on my playtime, I felt compensated by my progress. Still, I felt cheated at times. My friends were outside whooping it up, playing games and roller-skating, while I was cooped up studying. But I always respected my father's wishes, which I knew were for my own good. But my mother felt sorry for me and would yell out to my father from the kitchen, "Enough already with the singing. Let him go outside to his friends and get some air." Of course, my dad would finally give in, respecting my mother's wishes.

Henry Street always teemed with people and vendors. It was part of the East Side of New York at its best. There were the hot *knishes*, which were pieces of thin rolled dough folded over a filling such as mashed potatoes or chopped baked meat. Who could forget the large twisted pretzels, and Nathan's famous hot dogs with everything on them—pickles, onions, sauerkraut, and mustard. In summer, there were the vendors of flavored ices that cooled us down. In the winter, there were hot chestnuts with their rich aromas wafting through the air. I can taste it all now with relish. Nickels and even pennies went a long way then and we were able to buy many treats. Once in a while we bought "Break and Take," chocolate-covered mints, at the corner candy store. If the center was pink instead of white, we won a large chocolate bar—all for a penny. And who can forget when we ordered unflavored seltzer water, which we called "two cents plain." After the clerk served us, we asked him, "Maybe you could add a little chocolate syrup?" One pastry treat I savored was a "Charlotte Russe." It looked like an ice cream cone with a sponge cake base and topped with a swirl of whipped cream. Mmmmm, what a delight, and made only in New York City!

The most fascinating event to watch in those days was when a new tenant moved in. The movers were geniuses at getting furniture through the windows on the high tenement floors. I remember masses of people gathering on the streets to see if the pulleys would withstand the weight of the furniture. There were "oohs and aahs" from the onlookers when our piano was hoisted to the seventh floor window. When the movers succeeded in maneuvering it through, everyone yelled and applauded.

Summers in New York City were unbearably hot. Fire hydrants were opened so the kids could splash in the gushing water to stay cool. Those who couldn't afford bathing suits got wet in their underwear. For sure, it was no fashion show, but the kids had a great time screaming and splashing to their hearts' content.

In the middle of it all, the ice man cometh! There he was with his horse and wagon, ready to deliver ice to all the tenants. With great ease, he'd grasp a large block of ice with tongs, throw it over his shoulder which was covered with a thick matting, and stride into the building. I marveled at his strength, how he was able to carry the ice up to the seventh floor. Amazing! While he was delivering the ice, the other kids and I would jump onto the wagon and help ourselves to small ice chips. As it melted in our mouths, we delighted in its coldness. "Mmmm," everyone around us muttered as they licked their lips. We had to be careful, though, because the floor of the ice wagon was covered with coarse sawdust which sometimes became embedded in the ice.

As young children, my brothers and I harmonized together as we roamed the streets singing popular songs of the day. It was our dream to have the whole world hear us sing and not be limited to a local synagogue as cantors.

Miraculously, we were blessed with three different voice ranges. My older brother Murray was a high-pitched tenor, I was a lyric baritone with a tenor range, and my younger brother Phil possessed a low soothing baritone. Together, our harmony was unmatched as we sang songs varying from "The Hit Parade" to operatic arias.

Our family and most of our tenement neighbors lived on meager earnings, but we were rich in a spirit of sharing and camaraderie. When one of our neighbors was ill, my mother would bring chicken soup and other goodies. Other neighbors rushed in with home remedies, cleaned their house, and took care of the children. What an exciting world we lived in then! We learned the customs of the Italians, Greeks, Irish and Polish, while they in turn learned about Judaism from us. The building rocked with everyone's songs, from *"Sorrento"* to "When Irish Eyes Are Smiling," and from polkas to *"My Yiddishe Momme."* Education, the arts, the virtue of integrity, and the ethics of our fathers were stressed constantly by our parents.

New York's tenement districts were melting pots for immigrants of every faith, who all had the same mutual concerns and needs. The commandment "Love Thy Neighbor" was always paramount. In my mind, tenement living helped mold the foundation of my life. It was like a blueprint etched in my mind which helped design my character and outlook on life. Living around those wonderful and compassionate immigrants made us feel good; the atmosphere was filled with a rhythm and tempo that was exhilarating to everyone in the neighborhood.

It is my belief that the true architects of our great country were those early immigrants who dwelled among us. They filled our hearts with family values and meaning, and even taught us to appreciate more deeply the freedom we enjoy in America. As immigrants worked with zest and pride in their newly adopted country, they brought respect, warmth, and culture to the whole human family. I feel deeply that our country is a far better place because of its unique mixture of personalities and ethnicities from all parts of the world. Those first tenement dwellers, without malice or prejudice, loved and aided their fellow men and women. And they did it all with such grace, dignity and humility. What a blessing they were to the Lind family.

Our childhood was filled with song and happy days. Although we lacked material wealth, ours was a life rich in human values. The atmosphere that prevailed was all-encompassing in its warmth and passionate zest for living. The Synagogue filled our spiritual needs, and our parents enveloped us with their love and understanding. We respected and worshiped them as no others. Ever since I can remember, I was determined to make them proud of me. They had blessed me with the biblical name of David. I strove with all my heart to live up to its great heritage.

Chapter 2

IN THE BEGINNING

As a youngster, I was curious about my birth, on April Fool's Day, 1916. My father told me it was a very special day, because I was born on the holy Sabbath while he was chanting the morning services in his role as a cantor of a Brooklyn synagogue. One of his dearest friends had purposely delayed his usual early trek to the synagogue, waiting for the phone call from the hospital where I was born. When it finally came, he ran to the synagogue and did his good deed for the Sabbath by delivering the long-awaited message. He knew my father would be waiting on pins and needles worrying about Mom's health and the baby's condition. Now that Dad knew all was well, he beamed and continued chanting. He picked up the tempo of the liturgy he himself had composed, and finished the service in record time.

As he sat down in his special high-backed, extra-large, velvet-lined cantorial chair next to the holy Ark, the president of the congregation leaned over and whispered to my father, "What is it, Cantor? Your face is all flushed." When Dad told him the happy news, the president immediately walked toward the front of the pulpit, banged on the elevated lectern, and smiled. When everyone was brought to a hush he announced:

"It is my great pleasure to tell you that our esteemed Chazzan Yehoshua Lind has just had a second son!"

There was a loud murmuring as the entire congregation reacted joyfully. As the *Kohanim*, *Levites*, and *Israelites*, the descendants of particular tribes of Israel whose customs are carried on for generations by their offspring, were called up for their special participation in the

Joshua and Eva with newborn son, Murray, 1913

reading of the *Torah* scrolls, they shook my father's hands profusely and shouted, *"Mazel Tov!* Congratulations!"

My father told me that when he continued the last part of the Sabbath Morning Service, he chanted with such impassioned fervor that his tenor voice resounded through the walls, and must have traveled into the heavens themselves as he concluded with the rousing prayer, *"Adon Olom,"* "Lord of the World."

Anxious to get home, he rushed through the synagogue as congregants yelled their congratulations. In his dressing room he removed his silver-adorned prayer shawl quickly, kissing it as custom required as he laid it down. Then he gently removed his six-cornered cantorial hat. Under his long, black, flowing cantorial robe, he was drenched with perspiration. He rapidly donned a fresh flannel undershirt, while murmuring to himself, "What if this is an April Fool's joke? *Oy*, some joke." He reached the sidewalk with his handkerchief over his mouth so as not to catch cold in the chilly spring air, then walked briskly for six blocks to our home on Gates Avenue in Brooklyn, New York.

Mounting the steps leading to our apartment, he was greeted by well-wishing neighbors and friends who invited him in for *Kiddush*, the blessing chanted over the ceremonial wine. As the wine was poured and the blessings recited, everyone yelled, "*Lechayim—To Life!*" Then they served the traditional herring and sponge cake as my blessed father grinned with an inner glow that seemed to shine on everyone around him.

That afternoon, Dad could not relax or enjoy his usual Saturday afternoon nap. A hundred thoughts clouded his mind. He could not leave for the hospital until night descended and the Sabbath was over. He was anxious to see my mom, and me. So many things to discuss. there would be the traditional circumcision which was always performed on Jewish males on their eighth day of life. This sacred ritual would be carried out, as always, by a *mohel*, a religiously-trained and qualified circumcision surgeon.

When that special day arrived, as friends and family watched, the *mohel* prepared his surgical instruments and spread them out on a table nearby. My dear mother turned pale with fear. As she began to faint, friends quickly escorted her out of the room. After all, to a mother, even a minor surgical operation could be disastrous! In later years, I was told that when the *mohel* began the circumcision, I screamed my lungs out in protest . . . but all to deaf ears. All that our guests could say was, "Wow, does he have a voice." Already they were prejudiced and praising the power of my voice.

What would they name me? My father told me he had pondered this with Mom for days at the hospital. Finally he smiled and said, "*Chave*, why don't we call him *Dovid*? After all, he was born on the holy Sabbath, when we chant the Psalms of David. I have a feeling that God will bless him with a sweet voice, like he did King David."

My mom nodded approvingly as she agreed, "Yes, you're right, *Shiye*. He will be our *Dovidel*."

Now David took his place next to Moses, the first Lind son. Two years later, Mom left the celebration again as the *mohel* circumcised my younger brother, Phillip. After him, in two-year spans, sisters Norma and Selma joined the family. What a pleasure it was for Mom to finally bear girls and not have to go through the anxiety of circumcision.

It has always amazed me that for centuries, the legitimacy of circumcision has been debated. There has been constant controversy among laymen, doctors, and the religious hierarchy as they express their varied opinions as to why this custom is still followed by Jews and Muslims. As a Jew, I see it as a ritual that is accepted without question as an integral part of Judaism. Others see it as an antiquated, archaic practice that should be eliminated. Then there are those with the conviction that removing the foreskin is a positive hygienic way to avoid many communicative diseases.

This is a debate that will never be solved because of its ancient religious meaning. I have a question that I would like to pose about the timing of this ritual. I have a profound concern about inflicting such pain on a baby who is just eight days old. All of us know that we live in an imperfect world, that all of us suffer some kind of pain at times, albeit physical, mental, or because of some outside influence. As adults we accept that. But why is it necessary for an infant barely born into this world to suffer so much? No one but God, Who is the Creator of all life, can possibly know the effect or permanency of such pain inflicted on a mere child. Is this His law, or man's?

Chapter 3

My Cup Runneth Over— In My Father's House

My father ran a school for cantors. There were classes daily, and he would often end up writing during the wee hours of the morning. He composed liturgy for cantors and choral music for choir directors. When his students pleaded poverty, Dad would have my mother feed them and give them money to take the bus or train home. Then he'd hand them his music, accept their usual praise, and say, "You owe me." To him, money was always secondary, and that's why he had so little of it. "Money is not important," he'd say. People were more important.

Many have declared my father a true liturgical genius. Students were always lined up to study with him. To this day hundreds of singers, choir conductors, and cantors study and perform his works, which have been passed on from one to another without copyrights or royalties.

My parents' generosity didn't pertain only to money. Many times I'd wake up in the middle of the night and find myself on the bare floor. When I tried to return to my bed there would be some stranger in it, snoring away like an orchestra playing the "William Tell Overture." It was frustrating, but that was the way of our fathers. Still, I always felt sorry for my mother. I'll never know how she survived the freeloaders, the many artists, writers, and singers who always frequented our home, enjoying a free meal and a free place to stay. The weirdest scene was when foreign friends drank tea. Many of them would sip it through a lump of sugar held between their front teeth as they did in "the old country." The tea obviously tasted better that way, until their teeth rotted away. From then on, the sugar went into the glass.

There are other delicious memories that come to mind, especially about the Sabbath. On Fridays, Mom always scrubbed the floors of our apartment on her hands and knees, and scattered newspapers over them to keep them clean for the Sabbath. When we answered nature's call, we could sit in the bathroom and read the news of the day spread out on the floor. The house had a sweet freshness and the scent of the Sabbath holiness permeated the air, which always filled me with a sense of security.

There was a simplicity and quiet dignity in the preparation of the Sabbath table. It was set with our best dinnerware. At one end were the Sabbath candlesticks that Mom had brought over from her home in Rumania. Opposite the candlesticks, at the head of the table where Dad sat, was the large *challe* (breadloaf) twist, under a white linen cover embroidered with Jewish stars, *torahs* and other Jewish symbols. Kosher wine was in the center of the table, and my father's silver *Kiddush* cup, the ceremonial goblet for the blessing over the wine, was at his right.

The Friday night dinner was always something we looked forward to with relish. Mom prepared our favorite dishes. There was always the traditional chopped liver or *gefilte* fish, made of several different kinds of fish ground together, seasoned, and cooked in a broth. Then came the chicken noodle soup, which Mom filled with lima beans and carrots, followed by an entrée of chicken or beef.

The trimmings to the entrée were always one of the well-known gastronomical delights and much-enjoyed "three k's": *kishke* (casings of cow intestines stuffed with wonderful goodies), *kugel* (pudding), or *knishes* (Jewish ravioli). For a touch of color, Mom would make her specialty, tzimmes, a delicious mix of carrots, sweet potatoes, and prunes all roasted together in a sweet syrup. Our dessert was usually compote, made with dried apricots, raisins, and more prunes.

Our *Shabbes* meal was not over till we sang joyful Hebrew melodies with a lot of *bim-bams* (Jewish tra-la-la's), followed by laughter, chatter, and traditional honey cakes and sponge cakes. We sipped tea, seltzer and soft drinks and waited for our friends, neighbors, and relatives to drop in. No invitation was needed to join us for dessert.

In that era, visitors knew they were welcome at any time. Our families discussed the latest news and what was going on in our personal lives. Neighbors were friends and we considered them add-ons to our family. They genuinely cared, and had a great deal of compassion for all the family.

Sabbath to the Lind family was special and revered! We looked forward to our walk down Henry Street towards Dad's Synagogue, exchanging greetings with neighbors and friends as we neared the Henry Street Settlement House. Even non-Jewish neighbors would smile and shout greetings to us as we passed by.

As we entered the synagogue, congregants beamed as they anticipated our father's approach to the altar in his full cantorial regalia. When he finally walked down the aisle, all the chatting ceased. The audience was hushed and reverent, full of deep respect for their Cantor, whom they looked upon as their chosen messenger to God.

My father felt that his ultimate purpose was to bring spiritual inspiration and passion to the worshippers. Each time he chanted, he improvised and re-composed his own prepared musical phrases, bringing a greater depth to his cantillations. He was such a master of Hebrew interpretation that the ultra- learned and religious factions of the congregation would weave and bob their heads, turn their bodies from side to side, and actually lose themselves in the spirit of the prayers. It was as if Dad raised them to a new level of worship with his soul-singing, which was even more stunning when his choir chimed in with special background vocals that my father had composed for them.

When my brothers and I were old enough, usually when we reached the age of five, we, too, would be enlisted into the choir and eventually trained by Dad to be soloists. One *Kol Nidre,* the eve of the Yom Kippur holiday, my brother Murray fell ill with a terrible cold and had a temperature of 103 degrees. Dad was such a disciplinarian and positive thinker that he wrapped Murray in a blanket and actually carried him into the synagogue to sing his solos. All of this was done with Mom screaming her objections to no avail. To my father, duties to the congregation came first. During the Holy Sabbath and all the special holidays, he led hundreds of worshippers in prayer so they could dwell for a few hours with the Most High, in another world where earthly concerns came last. Sick or well, we were trained and dedicated to do our chanting, no matter what.

Of course, my mom did not see it that way. After all, she was our mother and deeply concerned about our health. She was furious with Dad when he insisted that Murray sing even though he was so ill! Mom felt our health was more important. Although Dad loved us equally, he felt that "the show must go on." His dedication to his synagogue was uppermost, and his faith was so strong that he knew in his heart that God would take care of Murray, of himself, of the choir, of everyone on the Holy Days. And when Murray quickly recovered, Dad knew he was right.

Mom never won any discussions with Dad when it came to his profession. But then she used to worry about him, too. "You work too hard," she would say to him, "especially with the children in the choir. You should rest more." His energy was indefatigable. He was such a perfectionist that it was either his way or no way when it came to the services. You could not change his mind once he said, "This is the way I want it!"

After the Sabbath, on Sundays, there were visits to the *Fareins* and *Farbands* (groups of Jewish immigrants from different areas of Eastern Europe). They were *Landsleit* (countrymen) who had come from the same villages or towns. These clans gathered in friendship and camaraderie, and raised money to help their own when they needed a job or a loan. They were always there for the poor and oppressed. Charity was the name of the game, one of the traditional tenets of Judaism. The amount of money they raised for charity was unbelievable! They gave and gave, even when they couldn't afford it.

During my father's years, cantors as a rule were not paid high salaries. Still, we never lacked for food, clothing, Hebrew schools, yeshivas, and other necessities. How did they do it? In a word: faith. That is what carried them through life. Any time Dad had a problem, he would look to the heavens and say, *"Gott vet helfen,"* "God will help," and God never failed him. Also, it didn't hurt that he had a wonderful sense of humor. My parents were always laughing—and we laughed with them.

Dad was also the most secure man I have ever known. He had faith, faith, and more faith in himself and in his God. He knew what his own capabilities were. He was so secure in his talent that he surrounded himself with the best singers he could find. Other cantors were not that secure when great singers vied for choral jobs in their temples. But Dad behaved differently. He felt that the better the choir, the better the service for his congregants. He knew his cantorial prowess was so powerful that another singer could never tread on his domain. He feared no one, and even wrote special solos for choir members with superior talent. As Dad added his unique cantillations and improvisations, the learned and aged synagogue members nodded in approval and awe, moaning, "*Oy*, how he can chant!"

One tenor soloist, by the name of Pinky Perlmut, had been turned down by other cantors because they feared him—he was just too good. My father hired him. Pinky, who could hit the high C's like Caruso, would become one of the most famous operatic tenors in the world. He was so outstanding that Dad wrote special solos for him . When Pinky sang a high C at the end of a choral number, backed up by a fabulous choir, there was a great buzz rarely heard in a congregation. Pinky later changed his name to Jan Peerce. Because Dad had given him a break in the choir and featured him as a soloist, Jan revered and admired my Dad for years and years to come. Some time later, Jan asked Dad to write some special Hebrew liturgy for him to use in concert. Jan's brother-in-law, Richard Tucker, who also made it to the Met, followed suit. When Dad started receiving royalties from Tucker's cantorial recordings, he was prouder than ever.

Many of my father's choir singers and soloists became successful in other ways. There was little Jackie Heller, who used Hebrew solos written for him by Dad to warm up backstage in theatres. Heller was quite famous in Vaudeville and nightclubs and ended up in Vegas permanently. Then there was David Sarnoff, who became president and founder of RCA, My dad touched the lives of many people, and some were kind enough to thank him. But their fame was the best thanks Dad could ever receive.

As for us, his children, it was the Fifth Commandment that we believed in. "Thanks" weren't enough! It was "Honor thy father and mother" that touched my parents more than anything. In a way, they honored *us* as well, just by being there when we needed them and serving as an example of how we should conduct our lives.

Chapter 4

BORN TO SING

After I completed all my studies with Dad, it was time to prove myself. I was only nine years old when I made my debut as a boy-cantor prodigy. Because Dad was busy with his own services, Mom had to escort me to the chosen synagogue. Even with her at my side, I was a bit apprehensive and tense as we joined worshipers rushing into the synagogue, as twilight descended and the Sabbath was about to begin.

I immediately headed for the clergy room to change into my specially-made cantorial garb. Then I entered the magnificent sanctuary of the congregation. The Jewish press had hailed my debut as a first in cantorial history, arousing the Jewish population to a heightened curiosity. As I stood at the back of the congregation, I could hear the murmurs of hundreds of people, all waiting for me to walk down the center aisle. I took a deep breath, held my head high, tucked my music book under my arm, and started walking.

As I neared the pulpit in the center of the sanctuary, I ascended a few steps to a high, wooden platform designed so everybody could see me. There was a hush in the congregation and I knew they were wondering if my voice was strong enough to lead so many people in prayer. In those days, sound systems were forbidden. Like at the opera, a cantor had to project, and to do that I would have had to study with opera teachers. But I was far too young to have done that kind of strenuous study. I had been taught voice and sight reading by my father for four years. Fortunately, I was a stocky kid with a powerful alto voice. Most synagogues were built of marble and wood, with great acoustics for vocalists. I was confident that my voice would carry throughout the sanctuary.

Applaudience: The Autobiography of Dale Lind

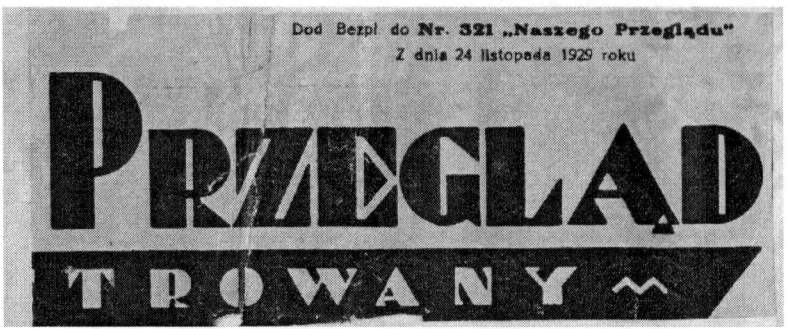

Newspapers worldwide picked up the Associated Press story; David as a cantorial prodigy at 9 years old, 1925

Now it was time to bellow the opening as loud as I could—six Hebrew words which meant, "Come, let us sing praises to the Lord!" Congregants bobbed their heads up and down in approval, their faces beaming with satisfaction. I felt encouraged, and continued in the same robust style.

I tried to find my Mom, but to no avail. Then I realized she was sitting behind a curtain that separated the men from the women, according to the custom of strict orthodoxy called *mechitze*. As I chanted on and on, I could feel beads of perspiration running down my face and under my arms. The experience of being a full-fledged cantor for the first time in my life was overwhelming. I began to tire after an hour and a half of nonstop singing. I started to worry about whether I could last through the wine service that would culminate the Friday evening service.

The service seemed endless. My heart was pounding faster than the tempo of the music. When I finally reached the wine service, the Sexton, with a great big smile of approval, handed me the traditional *Kiddish* cup filled with wine. The magnificent goblet, much larger than the one we had at home, was studded with garnet, green, and gold stones. It looked a hundred years old and weighed almost as much as I did. From the Sexton's smile I knew everyone was pleased so far with my performance. That gave me the confidence and energy I needed for my final chant.

I raised the enormous goblet with both hands and belted out in Hebrew, "Blessed art Thou, O Lord our God, Who created the fruit of the vine." I rushed through the last paragraph and before I knew it, I was at the end, singing the high note with gusto, and prolonging the last word, "Sabbath," to the full extent of my lungs! The whole congregation chimed in with a hearty *"O-Mein."* As the tension inside of me ebbed away, I felt like I was dying inside. I was exhausted and worried. Did they like me? Was I good enough? If I had failed, how could I face my dad? The congregation shocked me back into reality as applause rang out! I couldn't believe their reaction. Applause?? This was rarely condoned in a synagogue, but the voice of a nine-year-old child beseeching God in age-old prayers obviously had touched them beyond belief. I was honored and overwhelmed with all their praise.

As congregants rushed up to the pulpit yelling, "Congratulations," my mom watched, paralyzed. Then she pushed her way through the crowd and hugged and kissed me, as tears flowed down her face. My first words were, "Did I do good, Mom?" She hugged me again and said,

"You were more than good—you were wonderful! Wait till I tell Papa." I had passed my first test. I thanked God!

With my mother's arm around me, grasping me tightly, we headed back to the clergy room. I remembered my father's prophetic words, "Someday you will be a 'somebody' with no one ever again making fun of you or calling you a 'nobody.'"

As my fame grew, local newspapers wrote stories about me. Then a request came from the Associated Press for an interview. Naturally, my dad accepted and a time was arranged. My family was elated and excited. When a reporter and photographer showed up at our home, neighbors outside milled around the press car inquiring what was going on.

They had me pose in my cantorial regalia with my arms stretched out, like Al Jolson used to do when he sang "Mammy." It was so effective that my picture was in rotogravure sections throughout America, Canada and Europe.

I was eleven years old when Joseph Hyman, head of the Chicago Concert Bureau, flew to New York City to convince my parents that he should become my personal manager. I knew my folks would never deny me the marvelous experience of traveling throughout the country, and such a wonderful opportunity to win fame and fortune. Dad and Mom knew it would mean separation, but they finally agreed, as long as I would continue my schooling. Hyman promised to arrange for a private tutor for me. Mom decided to accompany me to Chicago to see that I settled in properly.

We said goodbye to our family and stepped onto the *20th Century Limited*. It was my first experience on a train. What an exciting trip that was! I had never eaten in a dining car or slept in a Pullman car. When it was bedtime, I climbed up to the top berth and Mom settled into the lower one. It was a real test of contortionism to get undressed on a speeding train, rocking to and fro. After bumping my head several times, I finally got under the sheets. The sound of the wheels on the tracks was rhythmic, and pretty soon I found myself beating out a railroad tempo as I fell into a deep slumber.

Chicago became my home for the next two years. From there I traveled throughout the Midwest, performing constantly.

About a year later, Hyman arranged an audition for me with vaudevillian George Jessel, who was breaking all attendance records at Chicago's Oriental Theatre. Jessel kept shaking his head as he listened to me. I thought he didn't like me. But when I finished singing "Under a Texas Moon" and Al Jolson's "Sonny Boy," he said, "Listen, kid, I want you on stage with me for the next show." He sent for the orchestra leader and told him to fake some background music. I was frightened. I couldn't imagine what it would be like to sing on such a mammoth vaudeville stage for such a vast audience.

When Jessel introduced me, I walked on to polite applause. The audience didn't know what to expect. It was so dark in the theatre that I couldn't see anyone. The bright spotlights on my face dazzled me, and I was petrified! Jessel gave me a grand introduction and smiled encouragingly as I walked towards the microphone. Inwardly, I prayed as I opened my mouth and heart and began singing. I was actually crying as I reached the last words of "Sonny Boy." Thunderous applause gave me new confidence. I then sang, "Under a Texas Moon." When I reached the last note, I held it as long as I could. The orchestra's trumpets blared, the timpani boomed, and I brought the house down.

Jessel put his arms around me and said, "You were great, kid." In the dressing room backstage, he talked to my manager about taking me on tour with him. Hyman said he would talk it over with my father, who wrote back incensed!

"What?! My son, a bum in Vaudeville? Never! For this I didn't send him to Chicago!" Suddenly my fleeting career in show business came to an end. It was back to the synagogue for me. After a few more months I returned home to New York and went back to school.

Some time later, I got a special thrill when Victor Records beckoned, asking me to record for them. My whole family was so excited when Dad went to Camden, New Jersey, to make the arrangements with Victor. Knowing that I would have to record some cantorial numbers with an organ accompaniment, Dad prepared the music.

When the editing was finished, my record was distributed to Jewish record stores everywhere. As speakers outside blared, playing my record along with those of other famous singers, my parents glowed with joy. Later, when Dad began receiving royalty checks, he was so excited he kept repeating, again and again, "Only in America could something so wonderful like this happen."

Chapter 5

My *Bar-Mitzvah* Day

It was easy for me to prepare for my *Bar-Mitzvah*, I was so fluent in the Hebrew and knew its translation because of my cantor-ing and yeshiva training.

Studying my special Sabbath *Haftorah* reading with the traditional "trop" melodies was like learning another cantorial retzetative. Still, I enjoyed the challenge along with my chanting, because it *was* my special day.

Meanwhile, dad had talked to his synagogue directors and they had decided to feature me as a guest cantor and to sell tickets for fifty cents, to attend my *Bar-Mitzvah* service. Synagogues always needed money, and this would give them another opportunity to raise some extra revenue.

As far as I know, this was the first time in synagogue history, and probably the last, that tickets were sold for a *Bar-Mitzvah*.

When my special day arrived, I chanted to an SRO crowd of over a thousand people. Worshipers from other synagogues had showed up in droves, as the Jewish press had alerted the entire Jewish community. Needless to say, my folks *kvelled* throughout the services as I sang my heart out. I was humbled by it all and gratified that my dad's *shul* benefitted from my big day.

I'll never forget my *Bar-Mitzvah*—it was a three day festival! Mom had been preparing food for weeks. Relatives and friends, some sleeping over for the weekend, carried on and ate like it was just after the Yom Kippur fast. It was like a giant food orgy.

Applaudience: The Autobiography of Dale Lind

David at age 13, 1929

Mom worked so hard preparing everything. The fact is, I never saw the day when my blessed mother didn't toil over household chores, cooking, baking, and entertaining Dad's numerous colleagues and friends. I received hundreds of presents. I ended up with twenty-three fountain pens, twelve watches, forty-nine 10-dollar gold pieces, ten bibles, six sets of the Books of Moses, three sets of *Tefilin*, (phylacteries: sacred objects worn on the forehead and arms during morning services), eight tie stickpins, and three gold rings. There were a hundred other items that we gave away to relatives and friends. The entire event was unbelievable and I knew I would never forget it.

Chapter 6

THE CRASH OF '29

A few weeks after the excitement died down, I began to feel restless and uneasy. There was an ominous feeling in the air. Then one night we heard a voice over the radio declare that the stock market had crashed. Newsboys were yelling in the streets, and panic set in as fortunes were wiped out.

The days that followed were sheer havoc. Friends and famous personalities committed suicide daily. At the time, I didn't think the tragedy would have any particular bearing on me, but it changed my life completely. None of us knew that Dad had invested all my earnings, which were considerable for those days. Under the management of the Chicago concert bureau, I had been earning $400 a week. Unfortunately, all of our savings had also gone into the markets. Suddenly he wasn't my jolly Pop anymore, but a tormented father worrying about our family. Now our nest-egg was all gone!

A few weeks later, a terrible commotion awakened me at about 5:00 A.M. I had an awful feeling that something horrible was happening. I ran into the living room and froze as I saw Murray and Phil grabbing and pulling at Dad. He was halfway out our second story window. Mom and my sisters, Norma and Selma, stood there crying and wringing their hands. The boys yelled to me, "Come on, help us—hurry, grab his legs and pull!"

Pop was so physically powerful that we were afraid he would pull away from us. We held onto him for dear life, screaming and crying desperately, "No, Pop, please, don't! We need you, we love you! Please, Pop!" Suddenly, he stopped fighting and collapsed into a chair. He was wan and exhausted.

Dad hadn't been able to sleep all night, so he had left his bed and put on his phylacteries. He was in the middle of his prayers when he panicked, lost complete control of his senses, and went for the window. I realize now, that the temperament of great artists is so powerful, their emotions so deep, that their reactions to catastrophes can be monumental. I had never seen my father cry before. As he sobbed, we all cried with him. He was filled with remorse, weeping uncontrollably. Finally he said, *"Oy, Kinderlach,* what are we going to do? The *shul* had to let me go. They can't afford my salary. The tears kept flowing as he looked up and said, "*Oy-oy-oy*—we'll starve. *Gotteniu*, God, why?"

Now Mama spoke. "Enough already. Come, Papa, I'll get you something hot to drink. The rest of you stop crying. Everything will be all right now." Mom was truly the heart of our household. God knows, we could never have survived the shock without her. That night I learned what it meant to have a strong mother—someone who was able to calm us down in any situation—and someone whose love made us feel all would be well.

As the years progressed, the effects of the depression began to fade, but I could never stop thinking of my father's desperation and near suicide. Subconsciously, I vowed that I would do everything in my power to avoid the kind of humiliation my dad had encountered when his synagogue fired him. How to do this? I would make myself indispensable to my employers so that they needed *me* more than I needed *them*. I would be as independent as my profession would allow me to be. I would never let anyone lord it over me...or fire me, as they had my dad. I was obsessed with a burning ambition to make good early in life so I could build on that in future years. I knew there would be bumps in the road to my independence, but I would never let myself waiver in my determination to overcome any challenges I would face.

Chapter 7

GREENER PASTURES

We tried to forget that terrible night after "The '29 Crash." Dad was still dazed and confused about the future. We were desperate! My brothers and I had to find a way to make a living. We put our heads together to find some way to merge our talents. After much deliberation, we hit on an inspiration! Wouldn't it be fantastic if we could form a quartet with our father? What a novelty our group could be. A father and three sons singing together would surely tug at everyone's heartstrings. True, we were in a nation-wide depression, but what Jew wouldn't buy a ticket to hear four cantors, all from one family? Together, we could become a sensation!

The thought of this gave Dad a new outlook on life. He began writing compositions for the four of us. Seeking to bring out the special qualities in each of us, he labored night and day to make this effort his best work. As he wrote, he began to be himself again. His whole attitude changed. He now had renewed faith and hope that we would bounce back financially, while winning national prominence as a family unit. It was good to see him jolly again. Our house was finally at peace.

Meanwhile, we had contacted my former manager in Chicago about our new idea. Hyman flipped for it. "Marvelous!" he exclaimed, "I can't wait to hear you together. This has to become the greatest Jewish attraction in history!"

As we discussed it more and more, we realized that Mom would have to travel with us. After all, she was our anchor in so many ways. Our food would have to be kosher, and that meant using our own dishes, utensils, and pots and pans. In the larger cities we would be able to find kosher restaurants, but not in every location. It would all be impossible without Mom. Besides, Dad would have it no other way. My sisters would have to stay with relatives so they could continue their schooling and that, too, had to be arranged.

Our manager wasted no time in setting up engagements in the Midwest, starting with a temporary contract in a large Detroit synagogue for the High Holidays. But there was a stipulation—we had to perform a Sabbath service first as a kind of introduction to the officers and members of the congregation.

CANTOR LIND
and His Three Sons

When we made our debut, our congregants went wild with delight. It was as we had predicted. They hired us immediately for the 1930 High Holy Days, only three days and two nights of singing, for the huge sum of four thousand dollars. In those days that was a small fortune. We no sooner deposited our earnings in a Detroit bank, when suddenly all the banks closed. To have another catastrophe so soon after the Wall Street crash put the whole country into chaos! Once again, we were broke, but so was everybody else in the nation. It was bedlam!

This time, instead of panicking, the entire situation struck us so funny that we began to laugh until we were hysterical. How could all this happen to us? It seemed so ridiculously funny. We emptied our pockets, put together our reserves, which was around ninety dollars, and bought sacks of onions, potatoes, bread, salamis, and all the necessities we could think of, so we wouldn't go hungry. This time we took it all in stride. We were assured by our bank that our money would be forthcoming, but it took years for them to dole out small amounts to depositors. We never did get it all, but we had enough to sustain us.

We also had help from the landlord of our building, who had become enamored with our family. He was wealthy, the president of our synagogue, and running for alderman of his district. He saw to it that there was always food on our table, which we appreciated. But there was a catch. He had two daughters whom he lauded as the most beautiful girls in the world. Not true! He kept hinting to my parents and to Murray and me that we would never have to worry financially if we would think about dating his daughters. Jewish parents were always natural *shadchans*, match-makers, whom I called "shotguns." Well, it didn't work. Murray and I were far too young to get involved. Besides, it was time to move on.

When the bank made another payment, we had enough to buy a used seven-passenger Cadillac, and decided to try our luck in greener pastures: Canada. It was winter, and there were seven of us in the car: my brothers and I, our parents, and two additional singers. All of us were wearing black fedora hats and black overcoats. Late one night, we pulled into a gas station to refuel. Everyone got out to stretch their legs. The gas station attendant took one look at the seven of us, and at our Illinois license plates, and panicked —thinking we were Chicago gangsters! He ran inside to his office and locked the door with a bang! As we stared at him, not understanding what was going on, he gestured that we should fill up our tank. It was an offer we couldn't refuse. "Wow," we said to each other, "We must have made quite an impression." Later, we realized what he had thought, and it struck us as very funny.

The winter roads were icy and hazardous. Murray, the eldest, was the only qualified driver, so all the responsibility for getting us to Toronto was on his shoulders. This was his first long journey, and he was rather nervous about it. All was going well until he erred in judgment as he started to pass a car on a very icy road. Suddenly another vehicle appeared out of nowhere, speeding toward us. Murray realized too late that he could not get back in time. He jammed on the brakes but we skidded badly, causing the oncoming truck to hit the rear end of our car. The impact was so powerful that we slid into a ditch and turned over six or seven times. Cars were tied up for miles. Many people left their cars, surrounded us, and began pulling us out of the ditch, wondering how many were killed.

Talk about providence—all seven of us crawled out unscathed. I remember thinking there must be someone "up there" watching over us. This was to be the forerunner of other such miracles. As time went on, I would be convinced that Fate played a definite part in my life.

I can't help but laugh now when I think that even in times of trouble there can also be humor. One of the extra singers, a friend of Dad's, kept yelling as we were lying in the ditch, "Oy, my tzitizen (citizen) papers, please, someone find my tzitizen papers. Dese Canadian police vill trow me in jail!" Well, that didn't happen; we found his papers.

Obviously, we survived our accident and managed to perform successfully throughout Canada. Most of our Canadian hosts in Toronto and Montreal were so touched by our singing family that they showered us with gifts.

After Canada we made our way to the West Coast, with appearances in Los Angeles, San Francisco, and Seattle, and then toured the Midwest, performing in Iowa, Nebraska, Ohio, and many other states on our way back to Chicago.

We had been traveling for several years with no real home to call our own. Growing tired of living out of a suitcase, Mom and Dad decided to settle down in Chicago. It was 1932 when Dad became the Cantor at the Austro-Galician Congregation on the Northwest Side. Chicago now became our permanent home. Although we would miss the exciting tempo of New York City living, Chicago had other advantages. As the nation's "Second City," Chicago offered a vast potential for our future. It was the heart and center of the USA. Chicago was warm and friendly and we quickly adjusted to its environment. It had the vibrancy of a big city combined with the cordiality of a small town. It was the consensus of Chicagoans that, "If you can't make it here, then you can't make it anywhere else."

Meanwhile, times changed. Show business was now acceptable, and Dad was suddenly determined to make good in Vaudeville. His colleague, Cantor Josef Rosenblatt, a renowned recording star who had also lost most of his money during the crash, was doing well in Vaudeville and beginning to recoup his fortune. As a boy of eleven, I had shared a bed with Cantor Rosenblatt when we were appearing in Chicago at the same time. We were both under the management of the Chicago Concert Bureau, and so we stayed at our manager's home. One night I couldn't sleep because I kept wondering if Cantor Rosenblatt would fall asleep with his beard under the covers or over them. I never found out, because I fell asleep as I waited for the great revelation.

When Cantor Rosenblatt consented to appear in Vaudeville, he was determined to recover his financial losses and redeem his honor by paying off his creditors in full. The only stipulation in his contract was that he would not appear during the Sabbath. That was a first in theatre history, and it brought him even greater approval and respect. Rosenblatt's success in the theatre inspired my dad to audition with us. Besides, we needed the money.

Chapter 8

THE CONGRESS THEATRE CAPER

In order to appear in Vaudeville, acts had to audition at a designated theatre where agents would be present to judge the merit of the act. We applied for this opportunity at one of the Balaban-Katz Theatres in Chicago and were given an audition date at the Congress Theatre on Milwaukee Avenue. This was a predominantly Polish neighborhood.

As act after act went on, Dad became more nervous. To enhance our act he had hired two more singers. One was a short, fat, gray-haired but mostly bald tenor in his sixties, and the other was an extremely tall, very skinny, mustached and goateed baritone in his thirties. We were to follow an accordionist who was "killing" the people with Polish polkas. Dad said to us, "*Oy*, if such an amateur can get a big hand like that, we'll steal the show." His words were prophetic but in a different way, for we were in the clutches of "The Congress Theatre Caper."

One of our numbers was a Hebrew religious song which could not be sung without *yarmulkes*, head coverings worn by religious Jews. At that time our cantorial hats were about six or seven inches high, and round. Because of their unique shape they had to be worn on the top of the head, overlapping a bit of the forehead.

When the stage manager cued us to go on, Dad arranged us in a straight line so he could face us while directing, with his back to the audience. Just as the curtain began to rise, it got stuck about twelve inches off the floor. We began running around yelling, "Bring up the curtain, bring up the curtain!" All the audience could see were feet rushing in different directions, and they began snickering. They presumed we were a comedy act, and their laughter built into guffaws.

When the curtain finally went all the way up, we must have been quite a sight, as Dad—a short, stout man—faced a motley group of five men who looked like a lineup at police headquarters. And that wasn't the worst of it—the audience took one look at the conglomeration of short, fat, and skinny singers wearing Chinese-looking skullcaps, and exploded with laughter!

We opened with "Song of the Flame," an adaptation of a Russian song. The first line was, "What's that light that is beckoning?" Pop's arrangement had four different singers each repeat the word "beckoning," one right after the other. The people laughed even more. When we finished the song, we got a huge round of applause.

Dad wanted our line to look proper while we sang. During the first number he had been pointing to those of us who were out of place, indicating where we needed to move. During the applause between numbers, one of us whispered to him not to point with his fingers, that it was rude.

Our second song was called "*Zmiros*," and was normally sung at home after the Sabbath dinner. My father turned white as he turned around to face the audience to announce our first Hebrew number. As they kept laughing he began to sweat and a multitude of thoughts ran through his mind. Now he was concerned that this non-Jewish audience might laugh even louder if he announced our song as the Hebrew "*Zmiros*." As the audience quieted down, Dad stared at them, terrified! I will never understand why Dad said what he did. He said only three words for his whole introduction, which he mumbled softly under his breath: "An Arabian Melody."

We broke up completely! Now the audience screamed at our reaction. Finally, we pulled ourselves together and began to sing.

"*Zmiros*" was the kind of melody where traditionally the words bim-bam-bim-bam would be interpolated into a Chassidic rhythm. Also, as in Swedish choirs, it was not unusual for choir boys to sing soprano. When Murray lost his alto voice three months before the High Holidays, Dad needed him desperately as a soloist. Dad was determined to develop Murray's head voice, and he successfully turned Murray into an amazing soprano. As Murray learned to sing intricate coloratura passages in his fantastic soprano voice, audiences were awed and dumbstruck with amazement.

But here we were in the Congress Theatre singing for a rough and tough audience busily eating popcorn and making quite a racket. As a result, when Murray started his solo and burst forth in a loud soprano voice with "bim-bam-bim-bam," the audience collapsed. As Murray realized they were laughing at him, tears began rolling down his face while he sang.

All of us turned red with embarrassment. On top of all this, Dad was flailing away with his hands, directing us like the famed Borah Minnevitch and his Harmonica Rascals. And not only that, but, remembering our advice, Dad kept indicating to us that we should straighten our line, by pointing with his *elbows*. The more he did that, the more the audience broke up.

After ten minutes of singing, we walked off to tremendous applause, which shocked us. Pop quickly motioned to Murray to return to the stage and sing an encore, "Ah, Sweet Mystery of Life." The audience kept yelling for more, and that was the only other number in our repertoire. I'll never forget the sad look on Murray's face as he looked at Dad and said, "What?! You want me to go out there *again*? Never! It's bad enough they think I'm queer!"

When we refused to do an encore, the audience reaction grew even louder. They yelled and screamed for more, but we had it. In a matter of seconds, Balaban and Katz agents were backstage congratulating all of us for a hilarious performance. When Dad heard them refer to us as a comedy act, he felt sick. When they urged us to call them the next day because they were definitely interested in booking us, Pop said, "What, we should appear as a comedy act? Forget it; we'd be criticized in every synagogue in the country. I'd be a laughing stock. *Oy*, what did I get myself into? Come on, kids, let's get out of here."

We left the theatre regretfully. When we got home we thought, "It wasn't so bad after all. We were pretty hilarious at that." But Pop wouldn't have it. His music was beautiful and sacred. A comedy act would bastardize everything he worked for. The money wasn't worth the shame. Dad lost heart; he was just too religious and too traditional. Back to the synagogue we went, where his labors would be revered and appreciated. His final words on the subject: "No more show business for me!!" From then on, it was only "*shul* business" for my Dad.

Chapter 9

A Century Of Progress (The World's Fair)

In 1932 and 1933, Chicago had its first World's Fair. "A Century of Progress" attracted people from all parts of the world to its exhibitions, futuristic architecture, and diverse entertainment.

Chicago's downtown "Loop" and Lake Shore Drive were literally manicured to perfection, as the city put on its best face for hundreds of thousands of tourists and proud Chicagoans. The myriad of attractions at the Lake Shore were hailed as a stunning display of the future. Corporations such as American Telephone and Telegraph, International Business Machines, General Electric, and General Motors were just a few of the industrial giants who presented their scientific innovations and wonders of things to come. Their exhibits were located near specially-built areas where entertainers and celebrities performed and shows were presented. Reporters roamed the golden shores of Lake Michigan, writing rave reviews of the city and the Fair.

Chicago was known for its hundreds of ethnic neighborhoods, and coordinators of the fair, as well as local politicos, made sure that most of them would be represented during special days and nights of the Fair. Italian, Polish, German, Jewish, and many other nationalities summoned their own entertainers to appear at Soldier Field, which seated more than 75,000 in its giant football arena. When my father, Murray, Phil and I were contacted to appear there along with many Hollywood and world celebrities on "Jewish Day," we were overcome with joy. This was the lift that Dad needed. It made him realize how powerful his name and fame was in the Jewish Community. He felt honored, respected, and appreciated, as all of us did. Inspired by it all, Dad composed a new arrangement of the famous Jewish lament, *"Eili Eili,"* "God, oh God, why hast Thou forsaken me?"

When Jewish Day finally arrived, with Jewish flags, posters, and decorations prominent throughout the area, we became even more excited. In a matter of minutes, we would be heading for the stage at Soldier Field to await our turn to perform. As stars from stage, screen, and radio preceded us, our anxiety grew to such a point that it was difficult to contain ourselves. When the moment finally arrived, it was awesome to hear the emcee announce: "Let us now welcome Chicago's own famed cantorial family, Cantor Joshua Lind and his three sons."

We had never faced such a massive audience: 75,000 people welcomed us with applause "from the roof tops." But that was just the introduction! Now it was time once again to live up to our reputation.

As we began singing, our voices soared through giant speakers that could be heard miles away along Michigan Avenue. The silence in the audience was amazing! There was no way of knowing how we were being received.

The climax of *"Eili Eili"* is the sacred prayer, *"Shema Yisroel."* The *"Shema"* is the prayer that a Jew is supposed to utter with his last breath on earth. It is the same message that is in the *mezuza*, a small, ornamental holder nailed to the doorposts of our homes, and the same words we proclaim again and again at all our religious services: "Hear Oh Israel, the Lord Our God, the Lord is One."

When our voices boomed to the heavens with those passionate words, our audience rose up with thunderous applause and cheered. We knew we would never, ever, hear such an ovation again. We just stood there—paralyzed and overwhelmed. It felt as if God's own voice sang through us that day. As long as I live, the memory of that performance with my father and brothers at Soldier Field will remain in my heart.

Chapter 10

NEW HORIZONS

In 1933, I chose opera as my desired goal. I sought out Chicago's best operatic and language teachers and began serious study for the next three years. At the end of that period, I began giving operatic recitals and appearing in concerts. I learned a great many arias and operatic scores. I mastered Italian, French, Spanish, and German arias, but I also loved singing every musical comedy song ever written, which extended my repertoire.

Living in an apartment above the Harmony Movie Theatre on Division Street was a lot of fun. While people waited in line to buy tickets for Nelson Eddy and Jeanette McDonald, they could hear us vocalizing upstairs. When we sang, "Ah, Sweet Mystery of Life," they thought it was from the movie soundtrack. Fortunately, the neighbors never complained. In fact, they loved it and asked us to keep singing—as if we'd ever quit!

A year later, everyone was congratulating us on Dad's new green neon sign, centered in the living room window. In that era, it was not considered bad taste to inform everyone, in any way, that you were a "Marriage Performer." Dad also advertised in the Jewish newspapers and gave out hundreds of business cards with his picture on them. The new sign however, was the "pièce de resistance"—quite an investment for Dad—which we hoped would pay off handsomely.

Big weddings were a rarity, and it was considered good luck to be married in the cantor's home. We had a large seven-room apartment, which was an ideal setting for a homespun wedding. When I think of the things Mom had to do to help Pop in his profession, I am humbled by it all. Naturally, we were all a part of it. While Mom prepared food and drinks, the rest of us pitched in whenever we could. We set the tables for the wedding feast, checked the wine and the canopy, and wrapped a glass in a napkin so it could be broken at the culmination of the ceremony, a ritual performed at every wedding in remembrance of the destruction of our temple in Jerusalem several thousand years ago.

During the summer, when it was extremely hot, there were more marriages than at other times. No one ever complained about the lack of air conditioning. Gentlemen removed their jackets, rolled up their shirt sleeves, and enjoyed every minute of the celebration. Beads of perspiration rolled down their faces as they drank "*Lechayim,*" and celebrated with great fervor.

While the ceremony was in progress, Murray usually accompanied Dad at the piano while Dad chanted and struggled through the English translation of the *Ketuba*, the Hebrew Marriage Contract. The "th's" were the hardest syllables for him to pronounce, but he never gave up trying.

Many times we acted as the choir for Dad while he sang. It wasn't important whether the clients paid for our services or not. They were in our home, and we wanted to make their wedding an unforgettable event. When our sisters Norma and Selma joined us, the guests raved even more about our harmony. The five of us were like a mini opera chorus, and the leading tenor—Dad—joined us for a rousing finish.

Many of Dad's colleagues were also Marriage Performers. The big three were Dad, Cantor Tevele Cohen, and Cantor Aaron Kritz. All of them did as many as six or seven weddings on Sundays, moving from place to place by cab. Followers were so loyal that they just waited until their particular cantor arrived and welcomed him even when he was hours late.

I remember one incident that floored all of us. The classic wedding song "Because" had replaced "Oh Promise Me" and had become the song for the bride as she stood in the aisle in all her glory. Not wanting to be outdone, all cantors began to sing "Because" in their ceremonies. One particular cantor had never taken the time to learn the proper pronunciation of the words. One Sunday afternoon, as he boomed out, "Mecause—you come on me . . . ." (instead of "Because—you come to me"), one of the guests, a doctor sitting on the sill of an open window, became hysterical with laughter. He began stuffing a handkerchief in his mouth to stifle his laughter. The more he thought about it, the more he wanted to scream out loud. Not wanting to disturb the ceremony, he rocked back and forth with silent laughter. Suddenly, leaning back too far, he fell out of the window to the lawn below. The ceremony continued as if nothing had happened. When it was over the cantor remarked, *"Der meshugener vos fell out di vinda is awright?"* He was simply asking if the nut who fell out the window was okay. Fortunately it was a ground floor and the doctor was not hurt. When the guests saw him on the grass, he was still exploding with laughter.

Musicians, many of them non-union, never made a big fuss about how many hours they played. They charged a flat rate and played until everyone went home, enjoying it as much as the guests did. They ate, drank, and were part of the family, and as a result they worked steadily and were in great demand.

Cantors, artists, photographers, and musicians gave of themselves without measure. They sang and played because they loved it, and did it with heart and soul. Money was always necessary and important, but it took second place to the genuineness of doing with pride what one was best trained for.

Many was the time when we were asked to sing for this or that purpose, such as an installation of synagogue officers, a memorial meeting, a banquet, a fund-raising event, or even at large card parties. It was done "gratis," and because of our loyalty there existed a brotherhood of fans who wouldn't think of celebrating any important wedding, *Bar-Mitzvah,* or occasion without us. Many times they forced cash into our pockets, which Dad ended up converting into a check for a wedding or *Bar-Mitzvah* present to the celebrants. It was a miracle how we always managed to eat and pay our bills with Dad giving away so much of his earnings. This made us even more determined to make good in a big way.

When Dad met a familiar face on the street, he would always say, "Let's go for coffee." In those days a cup of coffee cost five cents, but Dad would always leave the waiter a 25-cent tip. When we asked him, "Why so much?" Dad would always say, "He has to make a living." That was Dad, always feeling rich even though he wasn't. But, in another sense, he was very rich—with a great reputation, a loving family, and in a far better country than where he came from. He was grateful for America, and the freedom to do as he wished, and he let God know it every day of his life.

Chapter 11

STRANGE HAPPENINGS

Our family always "put on a happy face." No one ever knew what really went on behind the scenes unless we chose to tell them. As performers enjoying a certain amount of celebrity, it behooved us to keep our troubles to ourselves, and no one ever knew the reality of our unfulfilled dreams.

What we did know was our mission in life. Singing, chanting and entertaining—that was what we had to do, wanted to do, and were brought up to do. The love and appreciation showered upon us by the audiences we performed for helped us overcome many problems. On stage, it was always the applause that wrapped us in a coat of ecstacy. The warmth and praise that we received was an additional bonus for our efforts in bringing the kind of joy to audiences which was really an escape from the reality of life.

It was no surprise to my brothers and me when our dad did not reveal the financial problems he was having. It so happened one day, when we accidentally opened the mail and saw bills due from financial institutions, that we became aware of his problems. As the only wage-earner in our household, it was obvious to us that he had undertaken too many financial obligations and found them difficult to pay on a cantor's salary. He was using the "Peter-Paul" principle: he borrowed from Peter to pay Paul. Eventually he borrowed from a third institution to pay off the other two. It was a real mess.

When we approached Mom about Dad's situation, she told us everything because she was deeply concerned and regarded us as young adults, old enough to know what was going on. It was 1935; Murray was approaching 22, I was almost 19, and Phil was approaching 17. None of us were contributing any money to our folks because we had no jobs. After all, we were a sizeable family with seven people to feed and clothe. There were many other expenses like our education at *yeshivas*, institutions of higher learning, and the general home expenses of rent, utilities and much more.

Actually, the whole revelation came at a very appropriate time, because, unknown to us, a strange destiny was awaiting us. My father had a very close friend and colleague, Cantor Anshel Friedman, who had just returned from Israel. He excitedly told Dad that his daughter and her new Israeli husband, Kalman Aharoni, were coming to America to live and work here. Known as an astute businessman, Aharoni was offered the middle-western managership of the Schiff Shoe chain, for an extraordinary salary. The owners of the company gave him full authority to hire and fire employees at the company headquarters in Toledo, Ohio. A large part of his job was to seek out new talent to run their many stores. Qualified workers would be trained while working as assistant managers, and would eventually become managers in the growing company. Cantor Friedman wanted to know if my brothers and I would be interested, and told Dad it was a great opportunity to grow under his son-in-law's tutelage.

When Dad told us the news, all of us felt that we could not let this opportunity go—that this was a most timely event which would enable us to pay off Dad's debts. We all agreed to chance it.

Then Dad said, "Wait, boys. I have to tell you that I can't let all three of you go. I want Dave to stay and continue his vocal studies. His teachers told me that they foresee a great future for him and I don't think any of us should take away that opportunity. What do you both think?"

My brothers agreed that they would listen to Dad and let me stay, because they, too, believed in my future as a performer. But Dad didn't let it go at that. He added, "I don't want you to think that I favor Dave over you. I love you all equally. I just think that for now, Dave should have his chance to do what he does best." I was stunned by everything that was happening. I didn't know what to say. I kept thinking, "I better not disappoint my family."

My brothers called Cantor Friedman to intercede for them, and he told them, "You won't be sorry, boys. Kalman is a wonderful man who will also be your friend." When Murray and Phil were packed and ready to leave, we all hugged each other. My parents and sisters shed tears. All of us knew our home would never be the same again. I wept inwardly at our separation. It was all so sudden. Watching them get into the taxi and leave was like watching a movie. My brothers were off to an unknown future—without me.

As time went on, I felt awful that I wasn't contributing anything to our family. We were living in tough times, and there was always the need for more money. I was determined to do my part, and I began looking for a job. It was four weeks before Christmas, and stores in "the Loop" were hiring extra people.

Something within me led me to Marshall Field's. As I approached the hiring manager he took one look at me and said, "Do you need a job?"

I answered, "Yes." Right then and there he put me in the toy department in a booth selling "Talking Pictures." I hadn't even filled out an application! There was something he must have liked about me, or maybe they just needed more help. At any rate, it was the quickest result I ever received in an interview.

To get talking pictures from a toy was quite novel. As I turned a crank, a tiny movie, complete with sound track, appeared on the front of the toy box. Everyone was fascinated. I felt like a real hawker, as I yelled out, "Talking pictures—a new toy—come try it!" My trained voice echoed loudly to hundreds of people in the store, making the manager beam. I felt good that finally I was able to contribute my earnings to my parents. Both Dad and Mom were as proud of me as I was of myself.

When the holidays were over, the "sales" began. After a few weeks, my job was kaput. As it was, I had been neglecting my voice studies, so it was back to the studio for me, for good.

My singing teacher was Mario Rubini, formerly Morris Rubin. Having an Italian name was a great asset in those days, and it was common practice for opera students and teachers to alter their names. For a while I jokingly considered calling myself Davidello Lindenello! Rubini had a fabulous tenor voice, and had trained in Europe with the greatest opera stars. Even more than that, he was able to impart his knowledge to his students, using the traditional methods of Italian opera. When I began studying with him at age eighteen, my voice suddenly changed from a child to an adult, and that meant I had to learn a whole new way of projecting. As a child, I breathed and sang through my chest. Now Rubini was teaching me how to breathe and sing from my diaphragm.

That was not an easy progression to make. It took three years of serious study, followed by many more years of coaching, from the master himself. I had seen how Rubini took mediocre soprano voices, and after years of training, turned them into unbelievable sopranos. He accomplished miracles with me as well, which gave me the foundation for the vocal stamina I had for over 70 years.

Still, there was more to singing than just learning how to produce a beautiful sound. There was the feeling, the emotion behind it, that shaped the voice. As part of Rubini's teaching, he insisted that we listen to the recordings of the greatest singers of our era. I did that constantly at home. As I studied their technique, I realized that every singer of renown had a distinct quality of his own. When I listened to tenors Enrico Caruso and Benjamino Gigli, I was floored by the passion they exuded. It came from the depths of their souls and gave them a God-like quality as they sang. Lawrence Tibbet was an unbelievable lyric baritone whom I enjoyed immensely. The frivolity and lightheartedness of his Figaro in "The Barber of Seville" was delightful. In a sense, all of the great singers I listened to were also my teachers, and I tried to copy their different styles for different roles.

To me, dramatic operatic singing was like cantorial singing, where voices cry out with the pain and anguish of sorrowful situations. The voices of the great cantors always reflected the woes and tragedies of the Jewish people. The heart-breaking stories of the pogroms in Eastern Europe, anti-semitism, and the holocaust of World War II made their singing compelling and stunning, and touched the hearts of their listeners.

One day when I entered the studio, Rubini was walking on air. One of his star pupils, now using the stage name of Florence George, had won a contract for a starring role in a new movie in Hollywood. When other singing stars in Hollywood became aware of Florence's great voice, they urged her to convince Rubini to open a studio in Hollywood. It was a good move for Mario's career, and he relished it. Most of his Chicago students found new jobs in Los Angeles in order to continue their studies with him. As one of his star pupils, he urged me to come, too. Some of the male students were bunking together in apartments, as were the female students. Knowing it would certainly be a wonderful experience for me to see, meet, and hear other singing stars at work, I convinced my parents that I should leave for Hollywood. I knew it would be hard on my parents financially, so I turned to my brothers. Both of them agreed to pay for my living expenses every week. That cinched it, and I was on my way.

At Rubini's studio in Hollywood I met Florence George. We had been good friends in Chicago, and when she saw me, she hugged me and said she would arrange an audition for me with her husband, Everett Crosby, who was Bing's brother and manager. I always favored musical comedy, and at the audition I sang the well-known love song, "One Alone" from *The Desert Song,* in typical baritone style, with gusto. Crosby loved my voice, complimented me, and told me he could not represent me or any one else while he was Bing's manager. I don't think he would have even listened to me if Florence hadn't insisted. Frankly, I didn't blame him. Bing was a super-star! Why bother with me or any other singer? It was a mistake, but still a pleasant experience. I thanked Florence for her effort in my behalf and never saw her again.

After some months passed, I began getting antsy. It was 1937 and I was now 21 years old. I felt guilty that my brothers were still sending me their hard-earned money. I wondered how long it might take before I found the right agent, and even then there would be no guarantee of any kind of future in Hollywood. Should I return home? Maybe it was time.

My answer came quickly when I received a call from the president of a large Kansas City synagogue. He made me a very lucrative offer to chant the services for the High Holy Days. Naturally, I jumped at the opportunity and accepted his offer immediately. Besides, it was "pay-back time." This was the chance I was waiting for. When I arrived in Kansas City, something just didn't feel right. I knew my brothers missed their singing and had put all their hopes in me. Then it hit me! I would ask them to take a leave of absence from their employers (who were Jewish), with enough time to rehearse and sing with me for the holidays.

My brothers were elated! When I called Dad and told him the boys were joining me, he was overjoyed. It had bothered him, as it did me, that with such great voices, they were in Shoe Business instead of Shul Business.

Dad began composing some liturgical trios for us immediately. As it turned out, they were masterpieces. When we sang them for the first time on *Rosh Hashanah,* the Jewish New Year, the acceptance by the congregants was overwhelming. We were immediately offered another contract to appear for them in concert. We accepted and made our first attempt at arranging some American music as well. By including solo numbers we were able to work up enough repertoire for a two-hour concert. On the strength of our holiday appearance, the concert was a sellout. Our first trio number was a Victor Herbert medley, followed by an English-Italian version of "Vesti La Giubba" from the opera *Pagliacci*. Audience reaction built rapidly, and by the time we reached the *Pagliacci* finale, we received a standing ovation!

We were so delighted with our reception that we decided to work together as a trio. Now we knew that our real power lay in performing together. The people of Kansas City had given us our new purpose and, we hoped, a great career. After the concert we were too stimulated to sleep. We discussed our course of action in our hotel room until the wee hours of the morning. We all agreed that Chicago should be our prelude into show business. We had built a reputation in Chicago as cantors, and felt that Chicago was the place to begin our new career as entertainers.

We would realize that show business was a completely different animal. We would come to know many lean days and weeks as the doors of agents' offices closed in our faces. Having been brought up through a maze of ominous times, we had learned to shuck off disappointments. Although discouragement depressed us, we felt it would never defeat us. We encouraged each other and resolved to stick together no matter what! I felt like we were The Three Musketeers going into battle.

Meanwhile, our parents had moved to Denver, where Dad had accepted a great offer for a cantorial position. For us, it meant being on our own with an uncertain future. We knew it wasn't going to be easy, but we had faith in our uniqueness as a trio, and the determination to overcome any challenge. We rehearsed constantly, wrote our own arrangements, and worked on new material. We convinced ourselves that the Three Lind Brothers had what it takes, and kept a positive outlook that the right door would eventually open for us.

Chapter 12

A Miracle

We were broke most of the time. Money was scarce, and we were barely able to make ends meet. But we kept singing together and persisted in our determination to succeed. Once in a while, we performed services at different synagogues, and during the week we made daily rounds to different theatrical agents located in the Loop.

Meanwhile, the landlord of our building kept sending us notices for back rent. We were desperately trying to obtain some kind of singing break so we could pay off our obligations. We had too much pride to ask our parents for financial assistance. We owed everybody, including our milkman. Being an admirer of our father and feeling sorry for us, our milkman would leave milk, butter, eggs, and cheese at our door and never asked for payment.

Phil and I decided to talk to the landlord and ask him to be patient with us. We left Murray, our chef, to prepare dinner, and went up to Mr. Epstein's apartment. As we stood outside his door after ringing the bell, I began to get tense. I thought, "What if he evicts us, where will we go?" Mr. Epstein's voice resounded through the door as he yelled, "Come in, come in!"

He waved us on to where he was sitting and asked us to please sit down. We had never seen him before and I was struck by his holy appearance. He had a long, flowing white beard with Chasidic-curled sideburns. His silver gray hair around his pink face and deep blue eyes was so stunning that my tenseness eased. Suddenly, a deep calm enveloped me.

The aura of Mr. Epstein as I looked at him in his *yarmulke* was so filled with light that he looked *saintly*. As we sat down I noticed the book he was

Murray, Dale and Phil as cantors, 1938

reading was the *Talmud* (Jewish Law). Behind him on many shelves were books of theology, psychology, and Jewish literature. On another wall were Hebrew books on practically every facet of Jewish history. Special shelves were lined with Jewish artifacts, including sculptures of Moses, the Ten Commandments, the Torah, and the Prophets. It was an impressive display of what Judaism represented in our world.

Phil spoke first. "Mr. Epstein, you have been so patient with us that we want you to know how much we appreciate it." Epstein nodded. "We also want you to know that we would never have fallen behind in the rent if we had the money to pay you. The truth is, we are expecting some kind of break in show business any day now. It hasn't been easy for us. We have been making the rounds to agents and can't even afford the bus fare any more. Still, as desperate as we are, we are hopeful that a break will come soon. Mind you, we don't want you to think we've forsaken the synagogue as cantors. It's just that we feel we have too much talent to limit ourselves to synagogue chanting alone."

"If only the pressures weren't so great on us for money. We owe everyone—the butcher, the grocer, and the milkman. We really don't know where to turn. If our parents knew, they would probably insist on our returning home to them in Denver. Never have we tried so hard, rehearsed so much, and prayed so fervently to Almighty God to sustain our faith, hope, enthusiasm, and courage."

Epstein had listened intently to Phil. Now he turned to me. He stared at me with his penetrating eyes, and I blushed and became uneasy. Then he said, "Well, what about you? Do you wish to add anything to what your brother has told me?" An inspiration suddenly hit me.

I jumped up and said, "Mr. Epstein, while we're waiting for our big break we're negotiating with the KINS synagogue on Independence Boulevard and Thirteenth Street, to perform the Passover services. I would like to sing one of the melodies Dad wrote for us." I put my *yarmulke* on, blew my pitch pipe, and proceeded to chant a small portion of the holy prayer of *"Tal,"* a very dramatic prayer for ushering in the warm and rainy season.

As I began singing the traditional melodic strains, I could see it was affecting Epstein. After all, this was God's music. He began to move his head back and forth to the tempo of the melody I was chanting. When I reached the climax, he could not sit still. He jumped up and exclaimed with deep passion, "That was magnificent, I am truly touched!" He waited a minute and then said, "Now tell me, boys, do you have any money at all?"

"None," we answered.

"You mean not a cent?" he questioned us.

"That's right, Mr. Epstein. We're just flat broke."

Kalman Epstein commanded, "Esther darling, bring me my *tzedaka* (charity) box, please." His wife smiled as if she knew what her husband was about to do. She gave him the box. He opened it and withdrew a $50 bill. "Here, kids, buy yourselves some groceries. And when that runs out, come back for more. I don't want you to go hungry, ever."

Phil and I were speechless! We thanked him profusely. When we returned to our apartment and told Murray what happened, he said, "It's a miracle, a fantastic miracle!" It was an even greater miracle than we realized, for that $50 changed our whole life. *Mazel*—good luck—would now come our way in abundance, in the most bizarre way we could ever have imagined. I suspect that when we left Epstein, he prayed for us, as a holy man would.

A dear friend and colleague of my father, Cantor Tevele Cohen, had invited us for dinner at his home. Not wanting to spend our meager moneys on the "El," we decided to walk all the way. When we confessed to Cantor Cohen that we walked seven miles from the West Side to his home in Albany Park, that we were broke, Cohen was taken aback.

After he drove us home, he assured us he would get us some entertainment dates with some organizations in which he was active. Our first date, for which we received a grand total of $50, was a huge success. But even more important, we met a man there who had been doing a Vaudeville act for years. He was so impressed with our versatility and voices that he called us over to speak with him.

Chapter 13

CHICAGO'S HIGH-HAT CLUB: OUR DEBUT

He was an elderly man with a heart condition which forced him to retire from vaudeville. Obviously, in us, he saw himself starting all over again, so Benny Harrison became our good angel, and the kind of manager who was determined to get us a break in show business.

Benny knew all of the show business "*shtick*." One night, he said to us, "Kids, dress up in your best suits. We're going to Rush Street in the Loop. And oh, yes—bring your music." We couldn't imagine what he had in mind. When we reached Rush Street, we made our way to the Maryland Hotel. Benny said, "O.K., boys, this is where you stay till I return. Park yourselves in the lobby. I'm going to do my greatest selling job tonight."

We watched him walk across the street into the Hi-Hat Club, a well known nightclub in which many stars had appeared. Benny knew the owner only slightly, but he knew that he was Greek and loved opera. Benny was convinced that if the owner heard our arrangement of "*Pagliacci*," he would flip for us.

Benny told him he had secured a movie contract for us and that we were due in Hollywood in a few weeks. When the owner heard we were staying across the street at the Maryland Hotel, he pleaded with Benny to bring us over to sing in his club. At first, Benny acted reluctant, then finally consented.

When Benny reached us in the lobby, he was panting from running across the street. We were frightened because of his heart condition. As he sat down he was gasping for breath. After we brought him some water and he downed his nitro pills, he felt relieved. He filled us in on the details, and we rushed over to the club. Benny followed slowly.

When we finished rehearsing with the band backstage, the owner picked up the microphone, and with a great big smile introduced us as "three brothers on their way to Hollywood to make a movie." He added, "We are fortunate that their manager happened into our club and consented to their appearance tonight. Please join me in welcoming The Three Lind Brothers."

We opened to polite applause with the vocally-difficult "Donkey Serenade." In those days it was very unusual for a vocal group to display legitimate voices. Most of the groups were falsetto singers and crooners. Our opening song climaxed with a high finish, and the three of us gave it all we had. The audience was shocked at our voices and responded by giving us a big hand.

Our second number was a Victor Herbert medley, and then we were ready for the operatic *"Vesti La Giubba"* aria that the owner was waiting to hear. The kettle drums rolled, the big introduction ended, and I began the beautiful aria with *"Recitar."* Then Murray took over with *"E pour e duoppo,"* and Phil came in with his low solo at *"tu se Pagliacco."* So far, we had sung legitimately, as true opera singers. As we seguéd into a swing chorus of *"Vesti La Guibba,"* there was a murmur in the audience. As we got to the most thrilling passage, we dropped the swing version and harmonized *"Ridi Pagliacci"* with legitimate voices again. We could sense the full attention of the crowd, and to our surprise, everyone at the bar had stopped drinking. As we reached the final chords of *"Laugh, Clown, Laugh,"* the silence exploded into thunderous applause. People stood up, yelling, "More, more!" It was a fabulous debut for our first performance in a nightclub. The owner ran over to us and shook our hands. "Marvelous," he gushed. "Such magnificent voices!" Benny motioned to us to excuse ourselves. He told the owner we had to get our rest, and sent us back to The Maryland to wait for him. We knew he was going to press hard for some kind of engagement. This was our chance to break into show business in a big way.

Chicago's High-hat Club: Our Debut

Murray, Dale and Phil as entertainers, 1938

It took only thirty minutes. Benny came back, grinning widely. "Kids, you were great. You open tomorrow night at $250 a week for two weeks, with an option for another two weeks...if we can hold off the movie!"

We were dumbstruck! "Movie," we laughed, "What movie?"

It was a mad rush for us to open the very next night. Our repertoire was limited to one show, and at the Hi-Hat Club an act had to prepare for two different shows. We didn't have tuxes, so Benny loaned us some money. We bought three outfits—tails no less—for $22.50 each, at

Richman Brothers. We had been up half the night and were dead tired from figuring out some new routines. Then we retired and slept through the next day until 1:00 pm. That was the rest we needed.

On opening night all the newspaper critics were alerted to review the Hi-Hat's new act. The owner had invited them personally by phone. I was so nervous that I forgot to change the brown shoes I had been wearing with my street clothes. The critics were ecstatic anyway. Charlie Dawn of the *Herald-American* praised us highly, urging everyone to catch our act. One critic, after expressing his delight, wrote: "They must have been nervous, as the middle member wore brown shoes with his black tails." Maybe a new trend?

For once in our lives, our timing was right. Fortunately, Benny stayed alive long enough to help us get started. He died after our Hi-Hat engagement. But he lived long enough to see our first breakthrough. To us, he was like a messenger sent by God to open the doors for us to a new career and a new life. We would never forget him! What a wonderful soul he was. We prayed that God would reward him in Heaven!

Chapter 14

"SING & SWING UNLIMITED"

It was time for us to make some progressive moves in our career. It was 1939 and we were determined to get on radio. We arranged to audition for a Chicago network. Through a typographical error, when the announcer introduced us to the studio audience at our first audition, he called me "Dale" instead of "Dave." It had such a nice ring to it that I left it that way and eventually changed it legally.

Although the audition was a success, when the network discovered that we were cantors, it was "thumbs down," even though our repertoire for the radio wasn't Jewish. The network heads termed us a "Jewish act." In show business at that time, a label like that was instant death. After much thought, we decided to change our name temporarily to "The Noteworthies." In that way, we could overcome any bigotry. The psychological hang-up had been removed, and when we auditioned for WBBM, Chicago's CBS outlet, we were hired immediately.

Our first big show for them was "Sing and Swing Unlimited." Caesar Petrillo backed us up with a 35-piece orchestra containing some of the city's best musicians. There was Les Paul on guitar, Lionel Hampton on vibraphone, and many other greats who went on to become superstars. Our Sunday radio show was renewed again and again for two years. That gave us the opportunity to build a large library of new arrangements that served us well in future venues.

One day, an entertainment chairman for a large organization called and asked for the Lind Brothers. Phil answered the phone and negotiations for our appearance began. When Phil quoted our fee, the gentleman said, "Ridiculous. For that kind of money I can get The Noteworthies—radio stars."

Phil answered, "Go ahead and get them." The chairman called CBS and left his name for us to return his call. This time Murray took over, quoting fifty dollars higher than Phil had asked for. The man had no alternative but to accept. When Murray hung up, we howled! When we showed up at the affair, the chairman walked over disgustedly and said, "You're the Lind Brothers—we didn't hire you. What are you doing here?" When we told him we were also "The Noteworthies," he almost dropped dead. When the emcee informed our audience that "The Noteworthies" and "The Lind Brothers" were one and the same, the audience got a kick out of it and burst into applause. Appearing on radio under a different name did not diminish out status as cantors. In fact, those who discovered we were pursuing two careers at once only admired us more.

In those days, singing groups of three, four or more, huddled around one microphone and let the engineer in the sound booth handle the volume. Being the tallest Lind Brother, I was always in the center of our trio. I had to crouch down a bit so our voices would blend together in close harmony.

To make our performances more entertaining, CBS staff writers wrote scripts for us. Most of the time, when we read them at rehearsals, they were pretty awful. They were corny, not funny, and embarrassing. But we did the best we could with what we had and added our own lines as we went along. Staff writers were not professional comedy writers like those hired by big stars. Comedians like Jack Benny, George Burns and Gracie Allen, Fibber McGee and Molly, and Fred Allen hired the best writers they could find. Our forté was singing, and that made up for bad writing.

The funniest thing about radio was how everyone listened to their favorite shows. Families gathered together and stared at the radio—usually a fancy wooden box, as riotous laughter, mysteries, dramas, and music emanated from it. Radio was the main source of free entertainment

The Lind Brothers performing in Chicago with Eddie Cantor, 1940. Cantor was being honored for creating the March of Dimes to stamp out polio, which US President Franklin Delano Roosevelt and many others, were suffering from.

in the home, and everyone had a favorite program that all the family could enjoy together. God forbid if anyone used a foul word on radio. Even the simple word "damn" was forbidden by the network.

My brothers and I felt extremely lucky to be part of that wonderful era, especially when we guest-starred on Sid Caesar's Show of Shows, the Rudy Valee Show, the Chicago Theatre of the Air on WGN, and many other prime time presentations. Those were truly great moments in our careers.

Chapter 15

Chicago's West Side

It was 1940 when our folks decided to return to Chicago's West Side, which had become the largest Jewish area for Chicagoans and immigrants from every European country conceivable. My parents chose a large apartment on Douglas and Independence Boulevards, which was the heart of the Twenty-Fourth Ward and the Democratic stronghold of Chicago. The West Side was vast, going from Roosevelt Road to Whipple, east to Sacramento Boulevard, and south to Cermak Road. The northern boundary covered Central Park and Harrison Street. The southern areas also covered the Baltimore and Ohio Railroad area. There used to be a joke circulating in Chicago—that if you didn't vote Democratic in the Twenty-Fourth Ward, you got an eviction notice.

The Twenty-Fourth was also the home of Jack Arvey, the most powerful force in the Democratic Party. It was Arvey who convinced Adlai Stevenson to run for President of the United States. Later, when World War II was over, Arvey again tried for a Democrat to win the Presidency, and chose the very popular General Dwight D. Eisenhower. But the General turned Arvey down, and chose to run as a Republican!

Douglas Boulevard was also known as "Shul Row," with a synagogue on practically every block. A most unusual sight to watch, especially on Douglas Boulevard, was the parade of Jews on Friday at sunset, as worshippers hurried to their respective synagogues. Many dressed in their finest clothes to welcome the holy Sabbath. Others regarded the Sabbath as so sacred that they donned high hats, or as we called them, "stovepipes," to give the Shabbes special significance. Some looked like Abraham Lincoln in their beards and top hats.

Synagogues represented different parts of Europe from which immigrants had come. Through the years our family sang in most of them, so we learned to switch back and forth from *Ashkenazi* to *Sephardit* pronunciation. Jews belonged to the *shul* that most represented their customs and backgrounds, but they still frequented others to hear their favorite guest star cantors like Joseph Rosenblatt, Piérre Pinchuk, and Moshe Kousevitzky, all good friends of our father. As children, we knew them all, and I still remember their glorious voices and interpretations of the liturgy.

We were now living in our parents' home, and our cantorial trio was thriving. At the same time, we were appearing on CBS as "The Noteworthies," which most of our Jewish followers were not aware of. Hobnobbing with celebrities in our neighborhood was fascinating! A few doors away, there was the lightweight champion of the world, Barney Ross. Near him was the home of Abraham Lincoln Marovitz. Ross had also distinguished himself when he fought in World War II, winning medals as an outstanding marine, while Marovitz, a protégé of Jack Arvey, became a federal judge of great distinction.

The Lind Brothers were often called upon to entertain at political rallies, which were a boon to our career, especially when we sang for the first Mayor Richard Daley. As one of the most powerful mayors in the United States, he wielded tremendous influence in every facet of life in Chicago, and attracted huge crowds wherever he went. That didn't hurt us either!

The West Side was truly a throbbing community with a closely-knit way of life. Everyone shared the thrill of welcoming Jewish artists when they came to perform in the Douglas Park Yiddish Theatre. As they appeared in play after play, people laughed and cried accordingly. Many plots were similar; writers just gave them new titles with different twists here and there. As performers interpreted the roles differently, the plots seemed different to the audiences.

Audiences were constantly *"oy-vaying,"* as dramas unfolded about human failings, deep passions, and unrequited love. Parents on-stage berated their children who were marrying out of their faith, and praised their so-called good kids. Sometimes plots had parents condemning and disowning their children with their illegitimate babies. At other times there was extreme joy with weddings and other celebrations. It was truly amazing how Jewish plays were stereotyped. Still, we loved to watch the usual *yente*, who mixed into everyone's business. And of course, there was always the young romantic pair who tap-danced and sang their way into everyone's heart.

Chicago's Yiddish Theatre featured stars from New York's Second Avenue Theatre, which was home to big names like Leo Fuchs, Aaron Lebedeff, Maurice Schwartz, Molly Picon, Berta Gersten, Boris Thomashefsky, Dina Halperin, Hymie Jacobson and many other legends. Musicals were the most fun, as stars sang and danced to "Standing Room Only" crowds going wild with adoration.

Yiddish theatre playwrights were usually Shalom Aleichem imitations, so it was an amateurish "Fiddler on the Roof" every night. Yet it was all so alive and vibrant that today it is sorely missed by those of us who still remember that *haymishe*—warm, homey and friendly medium. In fact, it was so *haymish* that many stars always gave it a real personal touch at the end of the performance. Concerned with the play's successful run, a cast member would stand before the curtain and ask in Yiddish, "Well, my friends, how did you like the play?" Naturally, the audience applauded, then the stars would make their appeals: "Well then, please tell your friends what a great show you saw here tonight—that is if you liked it. If you didn't, tell them it was great anyway, so they will come and suffer like you did."

I particularly enjoyed watching Aaron Lebedeff perform. Russian Jews called him a *nazsh-brat,* a regular guy. He actually had ruptured himself several times in his anxiety to over-dance, over-acrobat, and over-sing in show after show. His zest left his audiences limp! When I heard him sing his own composition, the much-heralded "Rumania, Rumania," I promised myself that someday I, too, would sing it and record it for posterity.

Unfortunately, I never saw Edward G. Robinson or Muni Weisenfreund (Paul Muni) when they performed in New York's Yiddish theatre. My folks always talked about them, and when they became Hollywood stars, Jews throughout the country proudly flocked to theatres to claim them as their own. Yiddish theatre was a part of our culture, and most informative to other Americans of a European way of life that they would never have known otherwise.

In the summertime, Douglas Boulevard was a beehive. We'd join our tiny maternal grandmother, Mariasse Sonenschein, sitting on the stoop and watch what seemed like the whole world go by. Now a widow, Grandma had come all the way from Chernowitz, Rumania, to spend the rest of her life with us. She loved the Boulevard and had never seen so many Jews walking and conversing together with such great zest. Grandma spoke German fluently and was quite a cultured citizen in her Rumanian hometown of Bucovina. She cooked and sewed for us and was so proud of all of us. We dearly loved her.

On summer nights, families wandered around the neighborhood, meeting friends and joining them as they walked toward Roosevelt Road. In those days it was fun, just walking and talking. Everyone cared and was concerned about one another. The whole neighborhood bubbled with camaraderie. It didn't matter whether we were rich or poor, successful or not, we were all brothers and sisters and respected each other.

When we reached the always crowded Ye Olde Chocolate Shoppe on Roosevelt Road, we gorged ourselves with giant malteds and triple sundaes. From there, we'd go next door to see what the Central Park Theatre was featuring. I envied the headliners on the marquee. Inwardly, I hoped that some day our names would be up there, too. Six years later, in 1946, that hope came true.

Chapter 16

An Act Of Fate

My brothers and I had made a pact never to fall in love. We promised to stay single until we reached star status so that nothing would interfere with our careers. What a stupid pact it turned out to be, for we all found ourselves married within a few years.

In the meantime, a girl named Jessie Stemerman had left her hometown of Elmira, in upstate New York, to visit her brother and sister-in-law, Fran and Ida, who lived on the South Side of Chicago. After being urged to stay on, Jessie found employment almost immediately.

None of us could have ever anticipated that my youngest brother, Phil, would be the first to marry. A short time later, Murray followed suit. As the only single brother, I kept thinking "This is not good. Murray and Phil will now look at their lives and careers according to *their* needs and not mine. Being single will have its drawbacks."

Phil's wife to be, Rose Shapiro, began playing matchmaker. Through her family, she had met Jessie and decided she would make a perfect mate for me. Every time Rose and I were together, she, and later, her mother, too, kept pestering me with the same proverbial line that most Jewish mothers used on single men: *"Oy,* have I got a girl for you." Jewish women were born matchmakers!

Knowing that my brothers and I had a Sunday afternoon singing engagement, Rose invited us, as well as Jessie, to her mother's home for refreshments. This made it convenient for us to finally meet.

After singing engagements, we never indulged in ice cold drinks or anything that might affect our throats. Mrs. Shapiro, a gracious little lady, served us warm watermelon and sweets. Later I was told that Jessie thought we were weird. Who else could possibly eat warm watermelon?

I asked Jessie to join us as we headed for a movie. Afterwards, we made our way to the popular Batt's Jewish Style Restaurant, a little South of the Loop. All of us ordered deli-style sandwiches and drinks, and then I took Jessie home. When I said goodnight to her at the door of her house, I leaned over to kiss her. She turned away, rebuking me as she said, "Goodnight." I did not know then that a movie and dinner date in Elmira meant dinner and not sandwiches. Jessie thought I was a cheapskate!

I must admit that I was spoiled rotten. In the past I had never been refused a goodnight kiss. After all, I was a celebrity (big deal!), and well known to Chicago girls who sought me out. Jessie had bruised my ego. As a result I did not call her for months.

In those days, many "just marrieds" celebrated a special cake-cutting ceremony in their homes. Rose and Phil chose our parents' home shortly after their wedding and invited family and friends to their happy event. Of course, Fran and Ida, being related, were also invited. When they asked Jessie to join them, she refused, knowing I would be there. Fran and Ida then said to Jessie, "Well, we won't go either." That disturbed her no end. She loved them both. They were so good to her, so kind, so considerate. She changed her mind quickly and joined us at our home.

At the time, I was dating Florence Weiss, a 16-year-old heiress to an industrial fortune. I knew that she wasn't ready for any kind of serious relationship, but her family, who were involved with my synagogue, looked to the future. They invited me into their golf games even though I was a terrible golfer. They also invited me to see their warehouses and factories where they converted giant machines used for industrial purposes to meet special needs for the armed forces of our country. I was fascinated and quite impressed!

I had no inkling that Jessie would show up at the cake-cutting. It just never dawned on me. I had invited Florence, to our party, and when Jessie walked into our home, I turned red with embarrassment. In addition, her appearance was so exceptional that I did a double-take. I felt like lightning had struck me, and I thought, "What a dummy I am. How could I not have called her all this time?" As I approached her, I said, "Please don't leave early. I have to take my date home right after the cake-cutting, and it's a long way. I must talk to you."

When I returned, I made another date with Jessie, and this time we had a real dinner—no sandwiches!

Now Jessie had seen me in a different light, surrounded by family. Both of us sensed that we were ready for a more meaningful relationship. Fate had brought us together at a crucial time in my life, with our country already at war in Europe. I welcomed Jessie's friendship, and later, her love. Meanwhile, the draft was breathing down my neck, and the time for a new life in the military would be upon me.

It was Thanksgiving of 1942, just weeks away from my entering the Army, when I took Jessie to Chicago's famous Loop restaurant, Riccardo's. As a vegetarian, I used to frequent Riccardo's for their Italian food—the eggplant, pasta, and other vegetarian dishes. I also loved the warmth and intimacy of the place and the personnel. During dinner, the owner, Ric Riccardo, and the waiters sang all kinds of joyous songs, especially the funny "La Farfalla." We, too, joined other patrons in singing along. It was a unique evening in that I ate no meat, while Jessie celebrated Thanksgiving with the traditional turkey and all the trimmings. I must say I was tempted to join her, but our family had been vegetarians for five years, and meat was a "no-no."

It all started through friends of our family who were involved with some vegetarian groups. They painted a bleak picture of eating animal and poultry foods that had been slaughtered mercilessly by butchers. They convinced all of us that we would live a much healthier life eating fresh foods from the earth. Also, groceries and restaurants that featured only vegetarian foods were opening in Chicago's Loop, and were becoming quite popular throughout the country.

It was a great challenge for a Jewish family to give up so many traditional foods. But Mom owned up to the challenge by using certain ingredients that made it taste like the real thing. When my brother and sister-in-law, Ida and Fran Stemerman, were invited to our Passover Seder dinner, Ida was hilarious in the way she described it. She said, "We ate chopped liver that wasn't liver and poultry that wasn't chicken but tasted like duck that just wasn't. It was the craziest Seder dinner I ever ate. What a lifestyle!" We howled at her descriptions. Later, my brothers and I said, "You know what? Maybe we *are* crazy."

Riccardo's, with all its merriment, was the ideal place to give Jessie a gift. I had bought her a beautiful watch to show her that I really cared and was serious about our relationship. With my Army service about to begin, I was not ready to make any further commitment, not knowing how and where I was going to end up. I put the watch on her wrist at dessert time. As we looked into each other's eyes, we both knew that the day would come—I hoped—when I would ask her to become my wife. Because of all the uncertainty in my life, our future was put on "hold." I dreaded the thought of our upcoming separation. But I just wasn't ready . . . not yet!

After we were married, Jessie told me a funny story. After she moved to Chicago, and before she met me, she had gone to High Holiday services with a friend. As was the usual custom, they had gone from one shul to another, always sitting up in the balcony as orthodox laws required. Her friend had asked, "Have you ever heard of the Lind Brothers?"

"No," she replied.

"They're famous here. We'll go to hear them next." The girls then went to the Russian Shul on Douglas Boulevard. Jessie looked down from the balcony on "three guys in white satin robes, singing." After about 15 minutes, she said to her friend, "It's too hot in here, let's go." And they left. Jessie told me, laughing, "Little did I dream that someday I would have to tell you I walked out on you."

Chapter 17

SHOW TIME IN THE ARMY

There was a hush throughout our household as we listened to President Roosevelt on the radio speaking to the Congress of the United States. He declared that December 7, 1941, would go down in history as a "Day of Infamy." The Japanese had bombed Pearl Harbor in a sneak attack on Sunday morning, destroying our ships and personnel by the thousands! Suddenly all the bickering between political parties stopped, and all Americans united in a common cause: to rid the world of Japanese Imperialism. Our careers were temporarily halted as we, too, were caught up in the hysteria of revenge and patriotism.

We were tormented by the ugly thought of having to kill a human being. I couldn't even bring myself to kill a chicken. We were also very worried about being separated. We were determined to plead and beg the military to keep us together. We hoped the Army would keep us together if we could convince the right people that we could help morale by entertaining the troops as a trio.

It was Christmas time in 1942 when we were inducted at Camp Grant. Camp officers who had seen us perform recognized us and asked us to do some impromptu shows. We obliged gladly, hoping it would help us stay together. Meanwhile, we received a request from headquarters to attend a special meeting. We had no idea what the meeting was about. When we arrived, there was screen idol Cary Grant in the flesh. He was the star of stars—unbelievably handsome, immaculately dressed, and super-thin. He greeted us warmly and was as charming as anyone could be to three GIs. He then asked us to do a show with him and we jumped at the opportunity. We made certain to pose in a photograph with him which I treasure to this day!

Applaudience: The Autobiography of Dale Lind

Lind brothers with Cary Grant at Camp Grant, 1942

Performing with Grant for thousands of new inductees was a unique experience. He was the first movie star to appear with us and we were really excited. We opened the show with "Camptown Races" and then sang "The Donkey Serenade." Both songs were so well known that the huge audience whistled and screamed in approval. Still, our acceptance paled in comparison to the reception Grant received the moment he walked on stage. The entire audience stood up and cheered him even before he uttered one word. He was, after all, the number one star in Hollywood, and the audience showed him their appreciation for all the pleasure he had brought them through his various movie roles.

As he told stories about how it felt to work with superstars like Greta Garbo, Katharine Hepburn, and Ginger Rogers, he mesmerized the audience. In humorous asides, he told secrets about the business, such as when hidden cameras collapsed, falling on cast and crew, or props fell from heights into water pools that sizzled. The best stories, however, were about the love scenes he had faked. The audience laughed and shook their heads about how different it all looked on screen. When he remarked, after describing a love scene, "And we didn't even like each other," the GIs howled. "Think of what it feels like," he continued, "to kiss someone you can't stand." The audience ate it up. All in all, it was a wonderful performance, and we drank it all in with the rest of the crowd.

When shipping orders arrived, my brothers and I found that we were being shipped to Camp Claiborne, Louisiana, as a unit. We were delighted. So far, so good.

When we reported to the 103rd Infantry Division, we were immediately separated into different companies with each company destined for overseas duty in different areas. We were miserable as we feared permanent separation. We felt that as a group we could survive any situation. We also knew it was important that we continue to sing together in order to keep the blend and to continue to progress with new ideas and material. Three or four years away from each other could be disastrous, perhaps even end our professional career as a trio. We vowed with even greater determination to badger and hound camp and morale officers, as well as chaplains, into transferring us into the same company. It didn't work.

One unexpected problem was the food. As vegetarians, my brothers and I were really starving! All they gave us were potatoes and canned fruit salad, which we hated. We decided to talk to our chaplain. After hearing our complaint he simply said, "You're in the Army now, boys. You're going to have to change." And change we did. When we tried to eat chicken for the first time in years, we felt like we were eating a person, like cannibals.

One of the things that kept my own spirits high was that I was so deeply in love with Jessie. I kept her picture near me as I relaxed in my cot, thinking of her constantly. We had known each other for only three months, but during basic training I realized that I wanted her beside me for all of my life. I was depressed and lonely and so frightened of losing her to someone else that I had to do something about it immediately. I decided there was no way I was going to wait till after the war. I wrote and asked Jessie to join my sister-in-law Rose and come down for a camp visit. At the same time, I secretly asked Rose to purchase an engagement ring for me.

They finally arrived after a long, hot and terrible train trip overcrowded with soldiers, women, and children. On Valentine's Day, 1943, I asked her to marry me. I told her I was certain I could get a furlough after Basic Training. When she accepted my proposal, I was deliriously happy.

As far as I was concerned, military life stank. It was not as I had imagined. GIs who came from farms and small country towns adjusted to Army life far better than us city guys. They were used to getting up at 6:00 A.M. and they didn't mind retiring at 9:00 P.M. When "lights out" sounded, some of us headed for the latrines with our writing pads, taking advantage of the all-night lights to write to our wives and families. For a few hours, the latrines became our recreation rooms. Others wanted to shoot dice or play poker until the wee hours, and then went directly from the latrines to "Reveille." For certain, there were ringers, professional gamblers, who always stripped everyone of their money and sent that money home immediately.

In the minds of our Southern Non-Coms (Noncommissioned Officers), the Civil War was still on. They hated and resented us as Yanks and Northerners and were determined to make us miserable with continuous kitchen and other degrading duties. Checking our records and backgrounds, and seeing how successfully we were living life in the North, only made them more envious. Who knows, maybe being Jewish didn't help either. Just thinking about rejoining my family in Chicago for even a little while, and especially my forthcoming marriage, was exactly what I needed to make my military life bearable. I had to grin and bear it until finally basic training was over. My company commander graciously granted me the furlough he had promised me, and I left as soon as I could for home.

When I arrived home, I was shocked to see Jessie so thin. She had lost weight from the flu and was down to a mere 97 pounds. With the wedding only two days away, I was worried about her health. When her parents, Jake and Fanny Stemerman, flew in from Elmira, with many other relatives following, it perked Jessie up.

It was a delight to meet such *haymishe* folks, and I knew I had lucked out with Jessie's kin. She was the only girl among three brothers, Fran, Irv, and Bob, and I knew I had to do right by her or answer to them. At least, that's what they hinted to me in jest.

Talk about miracles! Bob was in the Air Corps and called us the day before the wedding to tell us that he couldn't get a pass to join us. But God works in strange ways, and the next day Bob was transferred to Chicago. To Jessie and me that was a miracle, and a good omen that all would go well in our marriage.

We were married by my father in his synagogue on the West Side of Chicago, on Independence Boulevard and Polk Street. The Rabbi of his shul, Saul Silver, also participated, as did both my brothers. Phil sang, "Because," and Murray sang, "Yours is My Heart Alone." We had our wedding dinner at the well-known Covenant Club, and we spent our honeymoon at the Graemere Hotel on the West Side. It was like leaving a hell-hole for a heavenly existence.

Chapter 18

WAR EXPERIENCES

When we returned to camp, my brothers and I resumed Army training. Jessie took a job working for the Civil Service at my camp, and I found a Jewish family who were willing to give her a room so she could be near me. Somehow, my brothers and I managed enough free time to put on shows, which endeared us to everyone. We were, therefore, quite shocked when we received special orders for a transfer to another camp. We had no idea why. Our transfer papers were being held up on purpose.

After many weeks, we were ordered to report to the Commanding General of the camp. We thought that finally we were going to be transferred together. After all, we had worked overtime to produce and direct shows, above and beyond the call of duty, and we expected to be shown some appreciation and be rewarded properly.

How wrong we were! We no more entered the General's private office when he started to chew us out. He gave us a vehement tongue lashing that I will never forget, and practically threw us out of the office. We looked at each other, shocked. Then Murray said, "What the hell did we do?"

When we returned to our respective companies, we heard that orders had been issued, from the General on down to our company commanders, to make it really tough on us. We were given every rotten detail that they could possibly devise. Against Army regulations we were put on kitchen police duty indefinitely, until we were ready to drop from heat prostration. When we were finally released from KP, we dug trenches and cleaned latrines for weeks. From there we graduated to polishing the floors of Officers' barracks and shining officers' boots. At night we fell into bed exhausted, depressed, and angry for being singled out.

We sought out officers and non-coms who had worked with us on shows from all the different companies, determined to find out why this was happening to us. After many days of probing, we discovered that the General had received "Red Borderline Orders" to transfer us to Fort Meade, Maryland. Those special orders would join us with others skilled in every possible kind of entertainment endeavor. We would be integrated into Special Service units, specifically designed to boost Army morale. It was extremely difficult to transfer GIs out of Infantry units, but Washington had lined those orders specifically in red, making it impossible for any Army officers to rescind.

Later, we found out that Washington had considered Army morale so important that they decided to enlist the aid of theatrical producers, such as the Shubert Brothers, who were given officer status. We were delighted to learn that the Shuberts were involved, as was Maurice Evans, the great Shakespearean actor, and many other show-business personalities.

Our Commanding General resented losing us to Special Services, and it was even worse when he thought we had personally arranged our transfer through our own civilian connections. He knew of our celebrity as civilians and thought we had pulled the proper strings. Later, he would discover that all personnel records were scanned by the Shuberts to specifically weed out the talent they needed to form these special units. In the meantime, we literally ate dirt, until they could detain us no longer. We were so dog-tired when the day of departure arrived; it was all we could do to drag our duffel bags to the waiting trucks.

Driving through the camp exit gates I looked up at Murray and Phil. None of us said a word. It was as if we could read each others' minds. We had just been through the blackest and most torturous weeks we had ever known. They had humiliated us, and we would never forget it. I had to say something to my brothers to cheer them up. "Well, it's over. After the rain comes sunshine." And so it did.

When we arrived at Fort Meade, a whole new world opened up to us. We became part of a professional team, along with movie projector operators, Post Exchange (PX) men, professional athletes, musicians, writers, and actors. From Hollywood, there was Sabu the Elephant Boy, former child-star Dickie Moore, and Bill Morrow, one of Bing Crosby's writers. In the sports department there was George Sisler, Jr., whose father was renowned as one of baseball's greatest first basemen. Musicians, singers, and dancers were everywhere. I felt like we were all assembled to put on a Broadway show.

In our barracks, Pete Seeger introduced himself to us. When we asked what his profession was, he picked up his guitar and said, "Just listen." And listen we did! We had never heard the kind of songs he sang. What a treat it was to listen to him. Everyone in the barracks gathered around as he sang the clever and funny songs he had written. We all broke up when he sang, "Rye Whiskey":

> Rye whiskey, rye whiskey, rye whiskey, I cry,
> If you don't give me rye whiskey, I surely will die.
> If the ocean was whiskey and I were a duck
> I'd swim to the bottom and never come up.
> Rye whiskey, rye whiskey, rye whiskey I cry.

The guffaws kept coming as he continued in his brilliant style. Now we knew why he was brought into our company.

And that wasn't all; there was a guy called Sam Messer, a strapping man with a great big bass voice. He was promoted to Sergeant and exercised his authority like a true leader. When he marched us around the camp, bellowing "Hut, 2, 3, 4" over and over, we didn't dare disobey. Trained originally as a Shakespearian actor, he made good in Hollywood after the war as a movie "heavy," performing with the likes of Humphrey Bogart and Edward G. Robinson. He changed his name to Robert Middleton and was quite successful in playing tough guys. He had the stature and the look of a mean character, snarling away with a big grin, making the audience cringe. In real life he was just the opposite—a wonderful, lovable human being whose friendship meant a great deal to us as civilians. I'll never forget him.

The most unusual meeting in our 39th Special Service Unit took place when a short, plump, studious-looking man approached us. A friendly GI introduced us and said, "Meet Jerry Siegel, the creator of 'Superman.'" He was the complete opposite of what his brain saw as the savior of our corrupt civilization. Later, as we became closer friends, we marveled as we watched him type new chapters of Superman with lightning speed. The words just poured out of him; he was amazing!

Some months later, Jerry was contacted by his partner, Jerry Schuster, with an offer from a large syndicate to buy the rights to Superman. Probably feeling like the rest of us, that the war would go on for years, they sold their comic strip for what was rumored to be a paltry sum. Little could any of us imagine that, in future years, Siegel would sue for millions when Superman became a movie headliner bringing in hundreds of millions to its producers.

A select few of us were chosen for very special recruiting missions. We were to attract crowds by entertaining and putting on shows wherever designated. By glamorizing the Army and entertaining our young people, we set out to sell patriotism. To our surprise, we ended up recruiting WACS (Women's Army Corps Service) in Cincinnati, Ohio. Our first gig was at People's Gas Company. We brought a portable piano right into the lobby, sang a few songs, and made a pitch for the young women to join up. Now we were all chanting, "What a war!" We were put up in hotels and given subsistence pay. I set up house with Jessie and we enjoyed three months of pure ecstasy, away from the camps.

We performed in theatres and vaudeville with Gene Autry and other stars. As we reveled in our new civilian surroundings, feeling good about ourselves and our good fortune, we could never have imagined the hell we would soon experience. Till now, the war existed only in our minds and our uniforms, but in a matter of weeks it would become a vivid reality.

When we returned to our company, they were already preparing for embarkment. We were informed that we would be heading to the South Pacific. We knew our honeymoon was over! Now reality set in as we shipped out to Hawaii for special training.

War Experiences

Entertaining with screen star Betty Hutton, 1944

Arriving in Pearl Harbor and seeing the sunken ships with their hulls protruding above the water was a horrible sight. We shuddered in the awesome quiet now reigning in the harbor. It was eerie, and I couldn't help thinking, "There but for the grace of God, go I." I sensed the stench of war as I envisioned so many of our ships being bombed by Japanese planes. They took such an awful toll. I certainly did not look forward to the conflict we would encounter. Just for a while, though, we would enjoy the atmosphere of Hawaii.

Training among the palm trees was a real picker-upper, almost like being on vacation. Hollywood stars were arriving in Hawaii to entertain the troops. Jack Benny came with his whole entourage, including singer Dennis Day (who later became our friend), Phil Harris, and Rochester. We didn't get to meet Benny due to army duties, but we did get acquainted with screen star Betty Hutton. She was a bundle of dynamite and a terrific performer. We were crazy about her. I wished we could have spent more time with her and gotten to know her better.

Surprisingly, our reputation as cantors had preceded us, and from time to time, Jewish Chaplains sought us out for special religious services. In Oahu, we chanted and co-conducted services on the High

Holidays with Rabbi Berman of Chicago and Rabbi Morris Adler of Detroit. They were fine gentlemen and a delight to work with. It was standing room only as Jewish personnel turned out for services in a High School auditorium. Every branch of the service was well-represented, and we reveled in the joy of doing what we could for so many lonely guys away from home. For us, it was the better part of war when so many of our fellow servicemen thanked us for reminding them of home.

During the services, I couldn't help thinking, "God knows what the future holds in store for us." Again and again , I posed the same questions in my mind. Why, when leaders of different nations do not agree, can't they find a saner solution than war? Where is their humanity? Why must they always go for the kill? When will our supposedly civilized world use the tools of peace rather than the arms of war? Are all these leaders crazy, power-hungry, maniacal fanatics who want only to impose their way as the right way? War is a sad commentary on our world leaders—who put their young in harm's way.

As we chanted away at the high school, our voices seemed different to me. The quality of our singing had a poignancy it had never had before. It was full of longing and solemnity, as if we were reaching out to the Eternal One for His protection and blessing as we prepared to join the fray in the South Pacific.

I felt a foreboding in the atmosphere, even though we tried to change the mood by singing some happy melodies to offset the more serious tone of the liturgy. More and more, I accepted the fact that it was our mission in the war to defray the somber and to bring some measure of joy and laughter to our buddies. I was glad that Murray, Phil and I could do that through our Special Service Unit. We were so lucky to be an integral part of that kind of mission and fulfillment.

Chapter 19

A Near Death Experience

It was the beginning of October, 1944, when we made our first landing on the island of Ulithi in the North Pacific, just east of the Philippines. GIs called it a real "hell-hole." The heat was intense, and we lacked any kind of refrigeration. Beer and cokes were consumed like hot soup, as perspiration soaked our bodies. Under such conditions regulations had to be relaxed. GIs went bare-chested all day as we inhabited this God-forsaken island for want of anything to do while waiting for moving orders. I was bored, hot, and sleepy. I sat down against a large tree stump. The terrain all around me was barren in spots, and dirty. I thought about home, the parks with their fresh greenery, and before I knew it, I fell into a deep slumber.

The dream I dreamed was so vivid that I remember it still. I found myself at Coney Island in New York City, sitting on the sandy beach watching the world go by. In one hand I held a cold drink, and in the other a "Nathan's" hot dog on which I munched with great relish. It had everything on it—sauerkraut, piccalilli, lettuce, tomato, mustard—the works. Teenagers in bathing suits were playing volleyball while younger children were splashing in the water, screaming as they threw a giant rubber ball to their elders. Thousands of people were strolling down the boardwalk as far as my eyes could see. It seemed never-ending. Bright colors were prevalent in green and red-striped awnings over the beach chairs, which were occupied by seniors eating fried chicken and other goodies. Sun bathers were reading newspapers and books, while children amused themselves with games and coloring books. There was laughter and noise in the air, and I loved every minute of it. I was still enjoying the panorama of the beach when some GI walked by me and accidentally kicked dirt in my face, waking me up. Result: dream over!

It was 5:00 a.m. one morning when sirens began wailing. We jumped from our bunks in wild confusion, sweating and wondering, "What now!" There was an ominous feeling in the air as GIs ran topside. My brothers and I grabbed our orchestrations and stuck them under our life belts as we, too, rushed up to the deck. It sounds ridiculous, but we had been in a deep sleep and could only think, "If the ship is sunk, our music will be lost." We weren't awake enough to realize that if the ship went down, we'd go with it! Meanwhile, a wise guy yelled, "Hey, Linds, what're you gonna do with your music now?!"

All hell broke loose as exploding ships and oil tankers catapulted GIs into fiery oil slicks. We felt helpless as we watched them burning in the water, screaming for help at the top of their lungs. Witnessing my first horror of the war, I felt revulsion and panic. I will never forget the sick odor on deck as guys threw up everywhere. Somebody yelled, "The poor bastards are being burned alive! Can't we do something?" Another answered, "How? Burn with them?" It was awful.

Obviously, the Japanese knew we were on our way to invade the Philippines. We were over a hundred ships strong, and part of General MacArthur's "I Shall Return" Army. This was the perfect set-up for Japanese submarines. They had maneuvered their one-man suicide subs through our radar by gliding in under our own ships as we entered the harbor.

By now some of our depth charges were taking their toll. As I caught my first glimpse of dead Japanese bodies floating to the surface amid enemy debris, I felt ill. Now the guys on my ship began cursing and hollering hysterically, "Kill the sons of bitches! Kill the bastards!" With my brothers standing next to me, I tried to keep my mind off the horror taking place around me by remembering how we tried to enlist in the Navy. We wanted to be part of Commander Eddie Peabody's unit because as an entertainer and banjoist, he knew the value of talent. He wielded great authority, and was given practically free reign to put together shows strictly for the entertainment of Navy personnel. As civilians, we were booked for a show by the William Morris Agency, at the Great Lakes Naval Station, with the fabulous Woody Herman Band. We were hoping our performance would convince Peabody to induct us into the Navy as a trio, which would keep us together throughout the war.

Commander Peabody was very pleased with our act and very complimentary. When we were ushered into his office the next day, Peabody looked grim. He said, "Look, fellows, I went to my highest authority and they refused my request for you. Their refusal was understandable, because it was based on the awful tragedy of the five Sullivan brothers who went down together on the same ship. They just won't take another risk by keeping you together. I suggest you take your chances with the Army."

Now, at Ulithi, I was wondering if it had been such a wise decision to stay together. I thought, "God, if we die together, our parents will never live through it." Phil held on to me, trembling, as more depth bombs were dropped. The yelling and screaming was deafening and seemed never-ending.

I turned my thoughts to Jessie. I could almost feel her near me, comforting me. She was an unusually beautiful woman. She was sensuous, warm, and breathtakingly exciting. From the moment we fell in love, I never wanted to leave her. She seemed a natural part of my life, and I loved her with my whole being. We were fortunate to have had fourteen months together in the States. For the usual fouled-up Army reasons, my brothers and I had taken Basic Training three times before going overseas. It was great that Jessie had managed to get civil service jobs in each camp so that we could enjoy some kind of marriage relationship.

I remembered how we had been pleasantly surprised when the Army ordered us to Dallas for a week. Jessie managed to get time off and went with us. When we arrived in Dallas, we received orders to report to their largest radio station. We had no inkling as to what our orders were all about. When we entered the studio, we couldn't believe our eyes, for there, in person, was Melvyn Douglas, the Hollywood screen idol! He was young and debonair and had a deep, majestic voice. He had just

Applaudience: The Autobiography of Dale Lind

Performing with screen star Melvyn Douglas, 1944

finished doing a movie with the fabulous Greta Garbo. He smiled as he shook our hands warmly and said, "Fellas, we're recording for the Armed forces. Here are your scripts, look them over. We record in an hour." Just like that, with little preparation, we began recording with Douglas.

When it was successfully completed he said, "Okay, guys, let's go to lunch." Jessie flipped when she was introduced to him. All through lunch she was completely absorbed and enamored with him. I became outrageously jealous and envious of Douglas. That night at our hotel, she kept repeating, "What a magnificent voice he has!" I couldn't resist answering her with, "Yes, but can he sing a high C?"

Douglas was extremely friendly to us, and after lunch invited us to his hotel suite for a drink. As he opened the door, he left it wide open. Then he began checking his closet, and looking under the bed. I thought, "What's he doing? Is he nuts?" We realized later he wasn't nuts, as he said to us, "You'd be amazed at what lengths some women will go to just to be with a celebrity." He gave us a valuable lesson for the future. We were grateful for a behind-the-scenes look at what goes on in the life of a superstar.

The sight of dead bodies and another enemy sub coming to the surface in pieces, snapped me back to reality. I was dizzy and sweaty. Fragments of my life floated in front of me. I couldn't help but wonder why I was suddenly thinking of Jess and home. Then I remembered Dad telling me that one's whole life flashes before him as death approaches. Was this what was happening to me? Was this going to be the end? I wanted to vomit. But suddenly a strange calm enveloped me and I thought, "Well, God, if this is it, then so be it."

Chapter 20

WHO SHALL LIVE AND WHO SHALL DIE

When the "All Clear" sounded we breathed a sigh of relief, and returned to our bunks. I was exhausted and felt limp after my first real war experience. I lay dazed on my cot, then Pete spoke to me. "Hey, Lind, for a while there I thought we were goners. . . ." I turned to look at him. Pete was always the happy one. I never knew what he was thinking behind his smiling facade. But now he was stark white!

I was afraid for him; I didn't know how deeply he was affected. I started talking to draw his attention away from what we had just witnessed. Pete, an atheist, was curious about my opinion of it. "Well, where was your God now, while they were blowing up our ships? How can you accept a God that allows innocent American kids to be blown up? How can anyone in their right mind believe there is a God that allows such carnage?"

Staring at him I said, "Look, I can't just give you a simple answer. If you want me to tell you my philosophy, why I believe in the existence and presence of God, I will. But I can't give you a quick answer unless you know something about my ideology. And it's not necessarily Jewish ideology. It's what I feel, myself." Everyone nearby looked at Pete as he said, "Okay, go ahead and convince me."

I decided to begin by trying to disprove his atheistic theories. "First of all, I know that you find it difficult to believe in anything you can't see or touch. But, for example, what about energy? Surely you believe in that, Pete, but you can't really see energy. Great scientists have probed beyond what they could see physically. Some of the most useful things in the world can't be seen. I feel that the unseen in our universe is far more powerful than that which we can see and touch."

"Let's take it a little further, Pete. Can you see your emotions? And don't say you don't have any, because you're still pale from what happened this morning. Emotions are a great part of our make-up, yet we can't see or touch them. Pete, we have to believe they exist because we feel them! It's the same way with God. Once you feel His existence, you believe in Him."

"As to *how* you can feel God, you have only to read the Bible to realize all the miracles He has performed, and the feeling will begin. Then look at the people around you and their lives. There are absolutely amazing coincidences that occur, and unbelievable strokes of luck that help people when they need it most. I have experienced these things in my own life. There is evidence of God's miracles."

"Believe me, He is everywhere, omnipresent, and in all of us. I assure you, the Good Lord did witness today's tragedy. But God never interferes in man's folly. In Jewish Scripture, we are told that when we are born we are given the gift of 'a free will.' We then can choose any course we please, good or evil, war or peace. True, war is hell, but it is a man-made hell, and we are bound by natural law to undo what we created. 'As we sow, so shall we reap.' "

At this point I was interrupted by encouragement from the guys. They were listening attentively. I could see that some of them really wanted to believe, so I continued. "Let's take a different direction. I'm sure you agree that doctors know fairly well what the human body consists of, right? And they know how it functions, right?"

"Right." Pete listened intently.

"Then *why can't they create a human being?* If man is merely a physical thing, organs and tissues and blood, they should be able to duplicate it, right? It's already possible to replace practically every vital organ we've got! But they *can't* create the original man, or his soul, and I assure you they never will. Only God can create the spirit that gives us Life. We ourselves are the greatest manifestation of HIM that was ever created." Pete nodded reluctantly. Now I was determined to explain my most important beliefs.

"I have always believed that no one really dies. It was only the bodies of those men that died today, not their souls. Those are of God Himself, eternal as the Sun. I truly believe in the reincarnation of man's soul. I feel that man returns again and again, in life after life, until he has fulfilled his specific purpose on Earth. Only then can the restlessness of man's spirit find true peace in his ultimate reward in Heaven. Our destiny and purpose guides us all, Pete, whether you believe it or not. If you can accept what I've just said, then many more things that happen in life make sense."

"Take Mozart, for instance. He was a genius, composing music at the age of five. At six, he was touring Europe as a concert pianist. He also taught himself how to play the violin and organ. Now I ask you, how is it humanly possible for a child of six to learn by himself what it takes an artist of great talent a lifetime to achieve? The only way I can explain such a phenomenon is to say that the soul of Wolfgang Mozart was obviously a lot older than six years. I have no doubt that his musical genius was inbred from another life."

"And another thing, many people are born with ESP, extra-sensory perception. Some can reveal the past and predict the future. Many police departments call on these gifted people to find a missing child or a murderer. That, too, is just another manifestation of God. It may sound weird, but try to understand that the wonder of God shows itself in many ways, through our spirit, and through nature, too. God's works are revealed in everything, in their proper Divine Order. To deny Him is to deny our own existence. I believe there is a Universal Plan for all life that is and ever will be. In our Jewish prayers, every year on the High Holidays, God decides, *"who shall live and who shall die."*

At this point, my mind was flooded with thoughts I wanted to express, especially after the horror we had just witnessed on deck. As I continued, everyone around me paid rapt attention. I asked a myriad of questions like, "Do you think our ship was spared today for no reason?" "Don't you wonder, sometimes, why someone standing near you gets hurt and you remain untouched?" "Do you really think everything that happens in life is accidental?"

And another question: "Why do so many athletes cross themselves before they go into action? Some of the greatest champions in the world, man or woman, depend on their faith to carry them through. I have watched boxers wear their faith around their necks, and heavyweight champions like Max Baer, who always wore a Jewish star on his trunks to denote his faith."

"If you believe in the Bible, there are so many miracles, like Moses parting the waters of the Red Sea to save the Jewish people from Pharoah. Or Abraham's arm being stopped by an angel from slaying his own son, Isaac, in faithful obedience to the Almighty's command to do so.

"Some of us who deeply believe in Him are shown the way God works in every instance. Strange as it may seem, He speaks to us in many ways through our minds, our actions, and yes, even our consciences—if we only listen. In our hearts, many of us can feel when we do God's will. Most of the time we succumb to human failings, perhaps for reasons that are emotional, psychological, or just unexplainable. In war, there are those who become heroes in a sudden act of bravery that they never anticipated they could do. I believe strongly that those who live on are meant to continue in life, perhaps to inspire others. And those who make the ultimate sacrifice are lifted up and embraced by God, Himself, for an eternal life of peace."

"I also believe that nothing in life is for nothing. Even the lowliest animal was forged by Him. Everything has a reason for being; the mountains, rivers and valleys exist for reasons that are unfathomable. To me, nature represents God, and when we go against nature, we will always pay the piper in some way."

There was total silence. I waited a second and added, "And now, if you don't mind, I'd like to get some sleep." I hadn't meant to sermonize, but the words seemed inspired by an Inner Voice. I was emotionally spent! The submarine attack made death very real as we watched those poor helpless kids dying. What an awful waste. . . and yet, was it not all preordained for those in our generation—who would be chosen to live, and who would become dead heroes? Who can ever know what awaits us in life? To me, every day that I wake is a great day!

As I closed my eyes, I pondered over my own destiny, I was grateful that my brothers and I were spared on this horrific day. I whispered, "Thank you God," and fell fast asleep.

Chapter 21

THE INVASION

We spent several more agonizing weeks at Ulithi, repairing the damage to some of our ships, before the order for the invasion of the Philippines came through. It was now October of 1944, and the rumor was that we were heading for Leyte Island. Because we were a specialized unit attached to Headquarters Company, we were in the rear echelon and spared the worst danger of moving in with the first wave of combat troops. That was usually done by the Marines.

Arriving at Leyte among an armada of battleships, we were in a position to observe what was happening on Leyte Beach. Our ships and planes were bombarding the island mercilessly. The fire and smoke were visible for miles. At the same time, we had the harrowing task of moving by rope ladder from our ship into landing crafts headed for Leyte. The waves were brutal, and the crafts kept smashing into the ship. We undertook this shaky operation with helmets on, back packs and other military paraphernalia. When my turn came to climb down the rope ladder, the GI beneath me slipped and fell into the water between the ship and the craft. My brother Phil was just steps above me. When he heard the GI scream, and saw a body splash into the water, he got panicky—he thought it was me! Phil had never learned to swim and was deathly afraid of the water, but I was his brother for God's sake—and drowning! Throwing all his fears to the wind, he jumped into the icy water. He held on to the landing craft, and almost drowning himself tried in vain to pull the body up. The craft was dangerously close to smashing into the ship. If Phil got wedged between the two, he would surely be crushed to a pulp.

Dale in uniform, 1943

The Lind Brothers in uniform, 1943

Fortunately, a few of the men in the craft acted in the nick of time. They reached out and pulled Phil up as he doggedly held on to the half-drowned GI, still thinking it was me. When he discovered he had rescued somebody else, he said in Yiddish, "A person could get killed around here!" I don't think he realized how comical his remark was. Did he say it to be funny? Was it a reflex? Was he serious? All I know is that those of us in the craft roared and it broke the tension of our mission.

Our company commander had been watching, and cited Phil for "courage and bravery beyond the call of duty." This earned Phil the Soldier's Medal as a war hero, which brought an eternal badge of honor and pride to our family. I still laugh when I think of what Phil said.

My dear brother acted—with no concern for his own life—to save *me* from possible death. It was a courageous act of love! For that, I salute him and will always be grateful. To my mind, there is no reward great enough for his noble deed. My love for him has no bounds.

When we finally reached the beachhead, dead bodies were strewn all over the area. The wrath and vengeance of our troops had been so severe that enemy bodies were unrecognizable. Penises and testicles were severed, and bodies were hacked in two. The dead had been robbed of watches, and rings were cut off with their fingers. It was degrading as hell, and I mused that even in death, there was nothing sacred in war. I didn't particularly enjoy being part of the winning team, but the alternative would have been a lot worse. I thought of my buddy Pete's words at Ulithi, when he asked me, "How can you believe in a God that allows such carnage?" But then I remembered the Bible quote, "An eye for an eye."

When the sirens went off on the island, we ran to the fox-holes. As we jumped in, we could hear the loud buzzing of our planes, heading towards the Japanese bombers. When the attacking planes went down in flames, it seemed like we were going to get hit by a wing, a wheel, or some part of the descending wreck. Some of the GI's were in a corner, praying. Others, like me, were watching the dog-fight. Although the machine guns were loud and seemed to be near, they were miles away. Still, there were bombs dropping, and no one knew where they would land. When the shooting ceased, the sirens blared again to let us know it was all over. When the army newspaper came out the next day, we were informed of how many enemy planes were destroyed.

It was amazing to me that we never lost a pilot. Were our pilots better than the Japanese? Who knows? Maybe they were just lucky. Whatever the case, during our time at Leyte, there were very few times when the alarms sounded, for which we were all grateful.

It was a solemn moment as General MacArthur walked towards the beach for the first time since his defeat. He had indeed "returned," as he had vowed, and we were now an integral part of history. The natives welcomed him ecstatically, cheering and yelling as they saw his familiar cap, sunglasses and pipe. Now they felt confident that the war would be won. When I saw their reaction, I, too, accepted our future victory more readily.

When things quieted down and the island was secure, we began to sing again, performing for the wounded in hospitals, which was sometimes disheartening, and doing special shows for officers and servicemen. It was good to be back in action again as a team. We built stages, sets, lights, and did shows whenever and wherever we could. One night we were driven to a camp in a rare blackout. When we reached the stage, there was still no sound indicating an audience. We were in complete darkness! Suddenly, as show time arrived, all the lights went on. We were flabbergasted—sitting in front of us, in total silence, were thousands of servicemen waiting patiently for the entertainment to begin. They were so appreciative that we exhausted ourselves with every routine we knew. It felt great to hear the band play Benny Goodman's "Sing, sing, sing." The GIs screamed, and some even got up and danced with each other. What a wonderful scene!

During the shows, I was always deathly afraid of snipers in the trees, watching our performances. The Army suspected that there were many of them, left behind when their armies scattered. They were probably right, for the cooks found food missing from time to time. One day, we found three of them in the chow lines, dressed in GI khakis, exhausted and hungry. They were almost happy to become our prisoners.

Native girls were all over the camp. It was easy to become acquainted with them. Their clothes were immaculately clean, and they were extremely friendly. They looked upon us as heroes. They were also marvelous at doing laundry, but when they came into the latrines looking for business, that was a little too much for me. For some, however, it did lower the barriers. The girls would shout, "Laundry, laundry!" and the GIs would get acquainted fast.

Because of loneliness and the great need for female companionship, romance flourished on the island. Most of the guys in my company were shacking up with native women. Some of them were exuberant when they became pregnant, because now they would have an "American souvenir." To them, that was the supreme blessing! *Oy vay!* Some souvenir!

Reveille on Leyte was at 6:00 A.M. It was always miserably cold in the mornings. I'd drag myself out of my cot and shiver in the chow line until I got a cup of hot coffee. Even powdered eggs tasted great, as long as they were hot. For sure, it was not a gourmet breakfast, but GIs accepted their lot cheerfully, especially as things calmed down after the invasion. Philippine natives were so happy to have us on the island that they invited us into their homes. They introduced us to delicious native foods and their specialty, fried bananas, which was absolutely delicious.

Now, once again we were back to our regular army duties. Being with my brothers had its disadvantages, too. Whenever they needed three guys for duties, the Sergeant would immediately yell, "Lind Brothers . . . ." We were well-liked though, and when there was an opening for one sergeancy, three stripes, they split it up and made each of us a private first class, with one stripe.

I hated guard duty most of all. The thought of walking around in the dead of night, alone, was horrifying. Four hours of guard duty was like an eternity, as my fear and imagination went into overtime. It was after midnight when I was on guard duty. One night, as I was walking my beat, I heard a rustling sound near a clump of bushes and was frightened out of my wits. I knew everyone in the company had checked in and was asleep. I cocked my rifle and yelled, "Who's there?" Someone shouted back instantly, "Don't shoot, we're friends!"

I thought, "My God, what if it's a ruse?" I imagined them overpowering me with knives, wounding or killing me. Three heavily armed Filipino guerrillas crawled out of the bushes slowly. My heart was in my mouth as they spoke.

"Take us to your company Commander." They were seeking shelter and food. I was relieved! The Captain fed them and set them up in a tent. I prayed I would never get guard duty again. I hated it!

And that wasn't all I hated. I was allergic to dust, which kept me sneezing on most days. When I reported for sick call, the doctor gave me an aspirin. No matter what a GI suffered from, the medics doled out aspirin as the perfect antidote. That was the cure-all. What a joke!

I had dreaded the war from the very beginning, living in constant fear of having to kill someone. My mother had taught us it was a sin to kill anything that had life, especially a human being. I didn't dare think of her reaction to what I had already witnessed. Soldiers killing and maiming other soldiers was not my idea of a civilized and humane way of life.

With talk of peace in the air, the USO began to saturate our area with top entertainers. When we heard that Danny Thomas was arriving in Leyte, we prepared to meet him. We had worked with Danny in Chicago at the 5100 Club and the Chez Paree, and knew he would be surprised to find us on the island. We left word with Headquarters to tell Danny where we were.

As we were going into our daily rehearsal with the band, we heard a familiar voice from the back of the room yell, "Do you think the rain will hurt the rhubarb?"

"Danny, you old son-of-a-gun!" We dropped our music and rushed over to him. He was wearing Army khakis, and had the familiar cigar in his mouth. He put his arms around all three of us, laughing and kidding and asking how we were. He looked great. Seeing him was like being back in Chicago again. He made arrangements immediately for us to appear with him. Danny pulverized our audiences, and we were a part of his thrilling triumph.

Working with Danny made me melancholy. Thoughts of Chicago and my family flooded my mind. I thought of Jessie and my folks, and I missed my sisters, too. I felt deep anguish for my sister Selma, who had just received news that her bombardier pilot husband was missing in action. They had been married only eleven months. She was pregnant, too, which made the shock even greater. Inwardly I mourned and prayed for her in her grief. What a tragedy for my baby sister. I regretted not being there to comfort her. I abhorred the war more than ever. Unfortunately, he was never found, and Selma had to wait five long years before his loss was made official.

Chapter 22

Kaye & Durocher

It was summer of 1945 when our camp buzzed with news of the arrival of Danny Kaye and Leo Durocher. Kaye was a Hollywood superstar, and Durocher was the fiery manager of the Brooklyn Dodgers. We had heard through the grapevine that they would need a band and additional acts to perform with them. We were keeping our fingers crossed. We had just seen Kaye's movie *Up in Arms,* and were looking for an opportunity to meet him. When word arrived that our act and band had been chosen to appear with him, we were thrilled. It also gave us a respite from camp.

Danny Kaye impressed us as being quiet and withdrawn off-stage. On the other hand, maybe he was just tired. Leo Durocher, however, was constantly kidding, outgoing and naturally funny. On stage, he would say things like: "If my own mother were playing for the opposition and rounding first base, I'd trip her." Leo proved he was really "The Lip," as he rambled on continuously with anecdotes about Babe Ruth, Lou Gehrig, and all of baseball's immortals.

Still, it was Kaye who was the true master showman. When he emerged on stage he was a fireball with unlimited energy. When he sang "Minnie the Moocher" and "Hip-ta-tiddy-ay" routines with his machine gun delivery, the GIs roared. And when Kaye coerced them into echoing his difficult lyrics, they broke up. He was a genius at involving his audiences, and we admired him for his superb showmanship.

He also drew tremendous laughs by joining the other acts on the bill. While we sang the "Whirling Dervish" and the "Hawaiian War Chant," he went into wild Oriental contortions with head and neck movements

Entertaining with Danny Kaye in the Philippines, 1943

that convulsed everyone. As we traveled with Danny, he warmed up to us, and we became good friends. We also found that we had a common bond, for he, too, had sung in synagogue choirs as a youngster in New York City.

Because some of our shows were scheduled at distant bases, a special plane was reserved for us. As Danny watched our plane being loaded with mammoth stage equipment, two pianos, band instruments, cast, and crew, he said, "Hell, I'm not flying in that thing. It'll never get off the ground." At first we thought he was joking, but when he and Durocher took off in the General's plane, we knew he wasn't kidding.

We left the runway with no problems. In fact, it was an extremely smooth take-off. We were almost at our destination when suddenly we were informed that we were lost. The pilot, in a desperate attempt to find

Lind Brothers and cast after plane crashed during World War II on the way to do a show with Danny Kaye, 1944

the runway, flew at a low altitude. When we spotted a runway, we were relieved. The pilot knew it was abandoned but decided to land anyway. Through neglect, the airfield was in terrible condition, and as we landed we hit a large object, overshot the field, and crashed into the rice paddies. The plane went over on its nose; our equipment broke loose from the ropes, and crashed into the lot of us. One of the pianos hit Phil, but he broke free of it as we nosed over. Someone kicked the emergency door open and we dragged each other out. Miraculously, no one was killed or wounded, but we ached for weeks from bruises everywhere.

As we pulled ourselves together, we made our way quickly to the nearest road and hailed some passing trucks. By the time we reached the base where Kaye and Durocher were nervously waiting, we were two hours late. When we told them what happened, Danny shouted, "I knew something would happen to that damn plane!"

I was still overwrought when we went into our routines. I kept thinking how lucky we were, walking away from a plane crash with no serious injuries. Surely heaven had smiled on us again. When we began our Olsen and Johnson routines, the exploding laughter eased our pain. I yelled, "Morning paper, get your morning paper," and Phil said, "Here, boy, I'll take the morning paper." Then I handed him a roll of toilet paper. Pretty corny, huh? But GIs loved that kind of humor.

Touring with Kaye and Durocher made me brood again for home. I became a bit depressed and impatient. The only thing that made it all tolerable was that I knew we would have enough points to ship home . My senses worked overtime as I imagined I was inhaling the Chicago air, and Jessie and I were walking along the lake. I could see her magnificent long auburn hair blowing in the wind as she put her hand in mine, and both of us would be in another world.

Chapter 23

COMMAND PERFORMANCE

Orders to leave the Philippines arrived in November of 1945, when we least expected it. Those who had sweethearts and wives bitched like crazy. Many of the men had made friends with the natives and their families, and were so entrenched on the Island that they never stopped to realize that their stay was only temporary. There was more sobbing and carrying on by the native women as we prepared to leave than there was during the Japanese occupation.

We suspected that we would be heading for Japan. Since the big bomb had been dropped on Hiroshima and Nagasaki, there had been continual talk of peace. When we heard of the havoc the atomic bombs had wrought, we all shared a common guilt. I kept imagining how horrible it would be if the enemy had dropped such a bomb on Chicago or New York. The thought of hundreds of thousands of innocent people killed or maimed for life, haunted me for a long time. What an awful way to stop the war. I couldn't help thinking that someone, someday, would have to "pay the piper." I must admit, however, that stopping the war—no matter how—probably saved thousands of American lives.

The sirens screamed and guns went off as radios blared the news of the Japanese surrender. Mass hysteria broke out and everyone was celebrating, dancing and singing. Emotions were out of control. When night descended, the sky was one large mass of every color of the rainbow as the "ack-ack" of guns and cannon shot at the stars. It was the greatest fireworks display I had ever seen. I thanked God they were fireworks of Peace. Then I thought, "Is it really over?"

When we entered the bay at Yokohama, no one was allowed to leave the ship. It was eerie as we looked at the landing ramps. There was no activity of any kind—just dead silence. My imagination worked overtime, and so did everyone else's. I thought "What if it's all a hoax? We'd make a helluva target in their home waters. This could be worse than Pearl Harbor." With thousands of ships and planes anchored in Yokohama and Tokyo Bay, this could be the greatest military catastrophe ever. Even though we were armed and prepared for any emergency, we felt like sitting ducks.

When the surrender was formally signed and we were ordered to disembark, our officers were still skeptical. We checked our carbines, and as I set foot on Japanese soil a quiver ran up and down my spine. I thought, "Is this really happening?" The area was still devoid of civilians. We went into formation and marched for several miles until the company reached a silk factory. This was to be converted into our headquarters. After the first night we had to break out our mosquito nets. The silk worms and bugs were biting us like crazy. We scratched until we were sore for days.

At the first opportunity, we emerged into the streets of Yokohama for our first look. Not knowing what to expect we moved in groups, as we were still afraid to trust the Japanese. When the civilians finally approached us, they kept bowing, as was their custom. It seemed like they were humbling themselves to their conquerors. Their humility disarmed us completely, and the hatred everyone had felt for so long suddenly turned to pity.

Tokyo overwhelmed me. It was so American in concept, yet sprinkled with its own culture. This blend was woven into every facet of their daily lives. I was amazed at how shopping in Tokyo was like shopping in any American city, with one exception: every other building was destroyed by our bombers and was now rubble. What an awesome sight!

We were scheduled to broadcast from a Tokyo radio station. The program would be beamed to all the Armed Forces. I thought we would be singing in a miniature radio station, as the Japanese were mostly short people. Their local trains were smaller than American trains, and I pictured us broadcasting from a tiny cubicle. I was embarrassingly wrong as we were ushered into a magnificent studio with every conceivable modern facility.

Now, with the war over, a black market flourished in Japan. Anything and everything was available for a price. Servicemen who were knowledgeable were trading in gems, and pearls were being purchased for ten cents on the dollar. Black marketeers traded U.S. merchandise, cigarettes, beer, and other PX inventory for jewelry and other luxuries. Japanese merchants, hungry for U.S. dollars and goods, were very happy to make trades.

Business was booming and the Ginza was like New York's Broadway at night. Dance halls and nightclubs were jammed with GIs and geishas. Tokyo was garish, happy, and wild with activity. It was a far cry from the hell-holes and misery we had endured for fifty-nine days on a Kaiser ship from Hawaii to the Philippines.

When my buddies left for the Red Light districts, they urged me to go with them. When I kept refusing they wondered if I was impotent. Being human, I was tempted to join them many times. But the constant thought that hounded me was Jessie's words during our last evening together. She had said, "Now honey, I know you're going overseas and you might be hungry for companionship. Do what you have to do, but for God's sake don't come home with a disease."

She had expressed herself so honestly that she had unknowingly put me on my honor. I was crawling up the walls, especially when my buddies discussed their experiences. But the possibility of contacting some kind of venereal disease repulsed me. Besides, my moral and religious ethics were so strong that I prayed for an inner strength to "lead me not into temptation."

It was a supreme thrill for us when we were invited to perform at the Imperial Palace. When our troupe arrived at the Palace gates, our special passes gave us entrée to a magnificent panorama. The grounds surrounding the Palace were breathtaking. The landscaping was flawless, like a Hollywood setting. We were especially excited at the prospect of seeing the Emperor. When he sat down in his special box, the atmosphere was charged with reverence. He cast an aura of sacredness and splendor, and all his subjects kept bowing in obedience. His uniform was regal, and his presence commanded respect and attention from everybody in the room. He was the divine symbol of survival and hope for his people.

During *our* show, our Imperial audience reacted with great appreciation and approval. Then it was their turn to entertain *us*. When Geishas walked out on stage in their colorful costumes and began their show with slow, calculated gyrations, we were all deeply affected. Wearing white chalk faces, they executed their movements with remarkable precision. Their Kabuki interpretations had such delicacy and dignity that we could only label them as Supreme Artists.

When we were fêted afterwards to a sumptuous supper, the geishas served us. They were everything we had read about: lovely, gentle, and dedicated to creating an atmosphere of warmth and comfort. We gazed at them constantly, in awe. They looked like toy dolls in Marshall Fields' windows—they did not seem real!

As the weeks flew by, my brothers and I were contacted by Rabbi Adler, with whom we had conducted services in Hawaii, to remind us that the High Holy Days were approaching and to invite us to conduct services with him in a Japanese chapel in Tokyo. This was another opportunity for us to lead the troops in prayer and thanksgiving for peace.

As army newspapers heralded our coming holiday services, all branches of the military were alerted. Our little chapel overflowed with Jewish servicemen from land and sea. They came in droves, and those who couldn't get in worshiped outside the chapel. We opened all the windows so everyone could participate. It was quite a sight to see so many Jewish GIs from all over the globe worshiping together.

Local Japanese Jews were also present. It was inconceivable to me that we could have Jewish Oriental ancestors. They were practicing orthodox Jews, and when we chanted the poignant *"Kol Nidre,"* the first prayer for on *Yom Kippur* night, they sobbed. Our congregants had never heard three cantorial voices chanting together in harmony. To see their reaction was another unforgettable experience.

Later, as the Japanese expressed their thanks and blessed us in Hebrew, we were again deeply touched. We also knew it would be the last important overseas service we would be chanting with Rabbi Adler, so we bade him farewell and promised to meet in the States. Unfortunately, that meeting never came to pass, for this great and wonderful human being, who had survived invasions and the holocaust of war, was murdered on his pulpit in Detroit.

It happened during Sabbath services, when a crazed young man stood up and pointed a gun towards the pulpit. Rabbi Adler, thinking only of the *Bar-Mitzvah* boy next to him, shielded him as the fatal shot rang out. Rabbi Adler slumped to the floor. He died as he had lived – in sacrifice. Indeed, it was his last, supreme act, for which his reward was surely "the Kingdom of Heaven."

Chapter 24

HOMEWARD BOUND

The shows we presented on Allied ships in Tokyo Bay were intensely gratifying. The Aussies (Australians) and British servicemen in the Japanese harbor were very receptive to our American songs and comedy. Their wild laughter and applause were great for our egos. Our act was really being put to the test because GIs did not have to be polite in their acceptance any longer. The three of us were overjoyed as they showered us with accolades, gifts, and the best in food that they had to offer. Moreover, we were rewarded with sergeant's stripes for our hard work entertaining the troops and boosting their morale.

As civilian life approached, my first thought was of Jessie. I wrote her of our embarking date and also sent word to a friend who had been corresponding with us throughout the war, Phil Shelley. Shelley was a Chicago agent who had been very successful in Hollywood and had expressed a desire to be our personal manager.

The day before we boarded ship to return home, I received a final letter from Jessie. She wrote that when I returned home she would have a "big surprise" for me. The thought of that big surprise haunted me from that day forward, and I was miserable all the way home. I kept thinking, "Maybe she's pregnant." After all, it had happened before, even to some of my buddies while they were overseas. Some of them even gave out cigars. A joke was making the rounds about one particular GI who was so proud he had become a father. When he was asked, "Hey, Joe, how could it be yours when you've been overseas for eighteen months," he answered indignantly, "Whaddaya mean? I wrote her every day." The obvious answer to that was, "What a pencil."

When we docked in San Diego four weeks later, I walked off the ramp, fell to the ground, and kissed it. I thought "God bless our American soil." There was no place like it, and it was all I could do to control myself. Inwardly I wept. It was so difficult to believe that I was home again.

My brothers and I had no more settled down in our temporary camp than we were paged on the telephone. It was Phil Shelley calling from Hollywood. He wanted to know if we could get a pass so he could treat us to a royal dinner. This was an invitation we weren't going to refuse. Somehow, we maneuvered a pass. When Shelley met us at the gate in his magnificent convertible, we were nonplussed. He looked great, and was dressed in typical Hollywood style: blue-checked sport coat, gold sport shirt, and powder-blue slacks. What a colorful change from army khaki.

Shelley had the body of a fighter. He was powerfully built, with square jaws and a bald head. We later discovered that he was a tyrant when he dealt with other agents and nightclub impresarios. He kept his acts working constantly as he bombarded buyers with wires and long distance calls. Although he was a dynamo as a salesman, he was gentle as a human being. It was always fun being with him, especially when we dined. He was a gourmet and loved to talk about exotic foods and good living. He was a romantic, loving nature and life. Most of all, he was dedicated to furthering the careers of his exclusively-managed acts. As a result, he handled only a handful of acts so he could concentrate only on them and keep them working full time. Personal managers received far more compensation than "ten percent agents" who represented hundreds of acts that could easily be overlooked. Shelley was worth every penny we paid him.

When we squabbled, as all group acts do, he would fly to whatever city we were performing in and bawl the hell out of us. "All right now, cut it out. You've worked too hard and have too good an act to be arguing." Then he would build up our egos and our hopes for the future. We came to love him as a second father, not just as a manager, because we knew he cared.

Our first dinner with Shelley was riotous. We were goggle-eyed when the waiter handed us the menu. It featured every conceivable delicacy one could desire. We were in a quandary as to what to order—after all, this was our first American restaurant in eighteen months! So Shelley, laughingly, helped us out. We ended up sharing each other's food and were so stuffed when we left that it was all we could do to *"shlep"* ourselves back to camp. After another meeting with Shelley we decided to entrust our future to him. We signed a long-term contract, and headed for home anxiously waiting for our first booking.

Before our dinner with Shelley, I had called Jessie from San Diego. The first words out of my mouth were, "What's the surprise?"

Jess answered, "Wait till you come home." I wanted to coax her into telling me, but it was impossible as other GIs were waiting for the telephone, and my three minutes were up.

Chapter 25

HOME AT LAST—FREE AGAIN

It was Christmas Eve, 1945. We were back at Camp Grant, where we had first donned Army uniforms. For a change, the Army pulled another snafu and fouled up Phil's discharge papers. We were quite upset and made the rounds of every important officer on duty. We had entered the Army together, survived together, and we were determined to muster out together. We knew our wives would be waiting at the station, along with our folks.

But we failed. As the train began pulling out, Murray and I were depressed until we saw Phil running like crazy to catch up to us. He was dragging his duffel bag through the snow and waving his discharge papers. We pulled him up just in time, and were happily three again.

We didn't shut up for a minute, all the way to Chicago. We fired up everyone on the train to join us in song. It was "Happy Days Are Here Again" and "Auld Lang Syne." Others were singing Christmas Carols as we pulled into Union Station.

My heart began thumping as I realized I'd be seeing my great love again in a matter of seconds. As we reached the gates we saw our wives, Jessie, Pearl, and Rose, standing side by side. There was a terrible snowstorm in Chicago. The girls had had a rough time getting to the depot, and our Mom and Dad didn't make it at all.

In a matter of minutes I was smothering Jessie with kisses. Everyone was embracing, and all of us were weeping. I thought my heart would burst. Suddenly I looked at Jess and she picked up my thoughts. She said, "Okay, okay. You want to know about my surprise. Well, honey, I gave up smoking."

"What?!"

"I gave up smoking because I knew how you hated it."

I stuttered and stammered and said, "G-G-Gee, honey, couldn't you have written me? I almost died of curiosity." While I chided her, I hated myself for thinking she might have been unfaithful.

It had started when she received my letter in which I had revealed, in code, our invasion plans for the Philippines. When she read about the invasion in the newspapers, the reality of it made her ill and she broke out in hives worrying about my safety. She had then made a vow that if I came through safely, she would give up something she enjoyed. She knew that her smoking bothered me because every night, when I returned to our hotel room after my nightclub shows, I complained that I reeked from smoke right through my underwear.

Now it was my turn to make a vow. I promised myself that I would shower Jess with all the love I was capable of, that I would never doubt her fidelity again, and that our marriage would be based on mutual trust and faith in one another.

In all of our more than 60 years of marriage, we have enjoyed a wonderful and fulfilling relationship. I think we found the secret ingredient, and it's that one important value: compassion. To appreciate one another's feelings with a profound understanding for one another's needs, and to nurture those needs with love and caring, made it all work for us. Learning to enjoy the same things, the same hobbies, the theatre, the arts, the friends we've enjoyed through the years, has always bolstered our interest in life. I think, too, it was following the examples set forth by our parents—their tenacity and their powerful faith—that gave us the courage to overcome our adversities. What better way is there to do that than to have a partner, a mate, to lean on and share all the burdens and successes together? In my eyes, no one in this life has a flawless existence. It is overcoming the bad times that makes us triumphant.

Chapter 26

THE *SCHVITZBUD* (SWEATBATH)

I felt polluted from the war, and I could think of no better place to relax and be cleansed than "the *Shvitz.*" This was a Russian-Turkish bathhouse that I had learned to enjoy with my father. Like many foreigners, Dad had always sought solace in the past, enjoying reminders of "the old country." When we were little, in New York, he took us to Libby's Bathhouse on Second Avenue. What a fantastic experience that was. In those days, the *Shvitz* at Libby's had a special room for "*Bonkes.*" This was a special healing process for all kinds of aches. As you lay on your stomach, empty glass bulbs were heated by a flame and placed on your back like suction cups. This was supposed to circulate the blood and cure you of all pains. It was a fascinating process to watch and undergo. My father loved it.

If that was too much of a chore, you could resort to the "needle showers" for instant circulation. As you stood there in your Adam and Eve get-up, someone would hold the hose and shoot it at you from a distance. The closer he came with the hose, the more the needle shower penetrated your body. I discovered that sometimes it hurts to be healthy.

In Chicago, Dad and I did our *shvitzing*, sweating, at Rosenberg's Luxor Baths on North Avenue. That was where I first learned that all men were not created equal. I had never seen such a conglomeration of protruding *poopiks* (belly buttons) in my life. In fact, they all looked like they were pregnant. It seemed like fat was in and skinny was out.

The camaraderie at the Shvitz had no equal. As we sat in the hot-room on the wooden benches in our nature suits or wearing sheets, the joking and ribbing was constant. There was no way of knowing who the strangers were; they could be doctors, lawyers, judges, or truck drivers. No one knew or cared at the schvitz, we were all human beings, and all one. Singers and cantors loved to show off their vocal prowess because the hot-room had great acoustics and voices sounded much bigger than they really were. I, for one, abstained because it seemed like a contest to me and I wasn't about to show off. Dad, who had taught some of the cantors present, just smiled and listened, above the fray. We just sat there, relaxed, and enjoyed the antics.

When it was our turn for a "*playtze,*" rubdown, on the top tier of the hot-room, the temperature was at least 170° F. The *playtze* was administered by a professional killer wielding a bush of oak leaves. In my opinion, those guys, who barely touched you, were true artists in the art of Russian massage. That was the massage to end all other scientific massages, and guaranteed to cure arthritis, rheumatism, and every other pain in your body, at least temporarily. Just when you thought you had enough, the heat-happy professional masseuse yelled to the person nearest to the oven door, "Pour some more water on the rocks. It's getting cold in here." Those were special rocks that sizzled with steam when water was poured over them. As the heat on our bodies became unbearable, someone would invariably yell, "close the damn oven door! You want to roast my *tuches* (rear end) off?"

Someone else would chime in with, "If this is what Hell is like, *Ich gay nit,*" "I'm not going!"

Another joker would say, "You think this is misery? You don't know my mother-in-law." On and on it went, the jokes, the wise-cracks, and the laughs. There was a rare equality here as all barriers were down.

My dad always ended up by saying, "Let's get out of here. These people are *meshuge,*" crazy, and we headed for the whirlpool. When the swirling waters engulfed our bodies, my dad would whisper under his breath, *"Oy, siz a mechaye,"* "It's such a delight." As he dunked himself again and again, he exuded sheer bliss.

After drying ourselves and donning fresh sheets, we proceeded upstairs to partake of the gastronomic wonders waiting for us in Dave Schaffel's restaurant. It was a Monday night ritual to be together with our "fellow-*shvitzers*" at a large banquet table laden with goodies! Dad and I relished the schmaltz herring as an appetizer. Next, I would order the mushroom barley or pea soup, while Dad ordered his favorite borscht with sour cream and a boiled potato. As the entrées began to arrive, we all lunged for our favorite dishes. There were salami and eggs, gefilte fish, kugels, salmon and chicken, with other treats fit for a king.

For his drink, Dad favored seltzer from a shpritz bottle, while others drank their pop or hot tea in a glass. It was a buffet to be proud of, with fruits and desserts a la Schaffel, who overfed our hunger with homemade delights. May God bless his memory!

I loved sharing and bonding with my dad. His rosy cheeks, good humor, and spiritual presence drew people to him no matter where he went. He loved to laugh, and when he did, his whole body shook with glee. He loved people and loved life in every aspect. He was a saintly man, and my teacher of ethics, music, and so much that mattered to me. I shall always carry him in my heart, for his wisdom, love and companionship.

Chapter 27

CLIMBING THE LADDER

As far as we were concerned, Phil Shelley was the greatest manager that ever lived. For our first booking out of the Army he secured a contract for $1,000 per week at Chicago's 5100 Club, the club that had catapulted Danny Thomas to fame. After the Army salary we had received, we felt like millionaires. During our first four-week engagement we did SRO (Standing Room Only) business. The critics sang our praises, and news of our success traveled throughout the nightclub world.

Shelley felt that now was the time to make our mark with bookings throughout the country. We needed critics and the press to write about us—stunning reviews, we hoped. *Variety*, the show biz "mag," had all the info on every act and how they fared in every city. Theatrical agents, club and theatre bookers followed *Variety* religiously as the Bible of show business, and we needed its recognition.

For several years we performed in the best clubs and theatres in the nation, as well as in Canada. Fortunately, we were "hot" and got rave reviews, with return engagements in most places. This was also how we became buddies with so many comics who sometimes shared billing with us. Many of them became superstars, including comedians like Alan King, Henny Youngman and Myron Cohen. Some of the clubs and theatres we enjoyed the most in Chicago were The Chicago Theatre, the Oriental Theatre, the 5100 Club, the Vine Gardens and the Mayfair Room at the Blackstone Hotel. Other bookings I remember as especially enjoyable were the Beverly Hills Country Club in Cincinnati, the Latin Quarter in New York, the Bradford Roof in Boston, the Normandy Roof in Montreal, the King George Hotel in Toronto, the Schroeder Hotel in

Milwaukee, the Frontier in Omaha, the King of Clubs in Portland, the Mark Hopkins Hotel in San Francisco, and the Chase Hotel in St. Louis.

On the strength of our tremendous acclaim, Shelley succeeded in booking us into New York City's plush Latin Quarter. This was a prime booking, as we would appear as part of a show led by Ted Lewis, one of the greatest entertainers in the business. He was a superstar and a living legend. We had never met him before and were anxious about his reaction to our act. The Latin Quarter was a large, rambling club, a real test for the talent and caliber of any act. We were determined to give it our all.

Our first three nights were extremely gratifying. Lewis liked us, and our performances were so well received that we felt secure and established as a professional act. Lou Walters, the producer and owner of the club, was the father of interviewer Barbara Walters. He was so pleased with our reception that we figured we'd stay with the show for months.

Our hopes for an extended stay at the Quarter turned into bitter disappointment after we spoke with Lewis' orchestra leader. He had been with Lewis for over twenty years and knew all his idiosyncrasies. He also knew his weaknesses. He told us, "You kids are just too good. Ted won't stand for it." We were shocked beyond belief! Everyone regarded Lewis as a class act as he performed in his tux with a cane and an old wrinkled top hat. He had become a show business legend with his recurring theme, "Is Everybody Happy?" My brothers and I wondered why such a big star would feel so threatened and insecure? We were so insignificant, and he was so famous. It didn't seem possible.

We had a definite contract for two weeks with a two-week option. Lewis never left the stage while we were performing. When we ran off after our last number, he would automatically go into his next number over our bows and applause, to keep us from doing an encore. We now knew that our option would never be picked up.

Night after night he got more upset as the audience applauded halfway through his number until he had to let us return for an encore. That made it even more definite that Walters would have to let us go. Lewis pulled all the *shtick* he knew, but we still finished our stint in a blaze of glory. When Phil Shelley heard what had happened, he was furious and more determined than ever to get us star billing so that no one could ever drag us down again. We began to realize that show-business was a dog-eat-dog business.

When *Variety,* the show business newspaper, raved about our act, Shelley succeeded in booking us into Slapsy Maxie's in Hollywood. It was a glamorous, sprawling nightclub named after ex-fighter Maxie Rosenblum. This was one of the fun bookings on the way up the ladder. It was big and important, with Hollywood agents and stars in attendance nightly.

The star of our show was Martha Raye, whom everybody loved. She was supported by such fabulous comedy stars as Ben Blue, Patty Moore, and Benny Lessy. Performing and just being part of this riotous show was a real privilege. We were with fantastic performers who made us feel like part of the family, and we learned a lot from their know-how.

Not only were we allowed to do our whole act, but we were also part of the finale of Martha Raye's act. For that portion we donned skin-tight White Guard uniforms and waved swords while doing a rousing chorus of the Musketeers. We concluded with the traditional goosing bit of Martha's act. The audience screamed at her lunatic reactions, with her big mouth and shocked expression, and finally fell off their seats convulsed with laughter. Martha was the epitome of comedy genius, and we were all crazy about her.

Off-stage she was charming, natural, and easy to be with. After every show, Martha joined her fellow actors in the audience, and was surrounded by admirers. I remember seeing comedian Jack Carson, Eddie Albert, Tony Martin, and Mel Torme smothering her with hugs and laughing out loud at her antics, jokes, and hilarious stories. One night Martha decided she wanted us to make a slight change in the finale. We had just shed our clothing and were relaxing, dripping wet, in our dressing room. She burst in unannounced! We scrambled for cover while she just stood there, laughing.

"For crying out loud," she yelled, "I've seen a lot more than you have." What a lunatic ... but so endearing. That was part of her charm and comedic outlook on life. We laughed with her as we doubled up!

Slapsie's was one of the most memorable and joyous bookings we ever had in a night club. It was also a learning experience in how to mesh together to make a successful show. I will never forget Martha's sidekicks: Ben Blue & Company. They got almost as many laughs as Martha did. I still remember his comedy *shtick* when he read a telegram he supposedly received from his wife, who was ill. He read it this way:

"Dear Ben. Not getting any better, come home at once." Lessey grabbed the telegram and said to Blue, "You're not reading it right. It says, "Not getting any—better come home at once." The audience screamed!

Chapter 28

STAR BILLING IN VEGAS, A FANTASY FULFILLED

As a direct result of our success at Slapsy Maxie's, we were contracted by Universal-International to appear in a movie musical short with Tommy Tucker and his band. In that era, musical shorts with famous bands were exceedingly popular. Audiences enjoyed them as "extra added" fare along with the featured movie.

It was thrilling and exciting for us to stroll around the Universal lot, surrounded by so many movie stars. It was a completely different atmosphere than theatres and clubs. It was magical in every way. As we went from set to set we felt as if we were in different worlds. Every studio created another atmosphere. We were astonished at the vastness of it all, from Westerns to mammoth epics and musical extravaganzas.

While we were lunching in the studio commissary, Eddie Albert walked by with Claudette Colbert. We were thrilled when he said hello, introduced us to Colbert, and told us that he had enjoyed our act at Slapsie's the night before. Miss Colbert was warm and friendly, as was everyone else we met. What a magic world that was, and how we wished we could be more involved in moving pictures.

When our movie, "Tommy Tucker Time," opened, the management of the Central Park Theatre on Chicago's West Side gave us top billing above Jimmy Cagney on the marquee! As far as the West Side of Chicago was concerned, we were the stars that week. Lines formed for blocks to herald us as their own. As for our parents, they were in another world, one of glory and new-found fame. They entered the theatre every day

Applaudience: The Autobiography of Dale Lind

The Lind Brothers singing to Marilyn Hare and orchestra leader Tommy Tucker in Universal Pictures musical featurette, 1947

with different friends. The manager admitted them free and gave them a big welcome! Everyone in the lobby congratulated them and wished them a great big *Mazel Tov.*

After we completed the movie, Shelley brought us more good news. He had booked us into the Flamingo in Las Vegas, where we would follow "the last of the red-hot mamas," Sophie Tucker. We had never worked in Vegas and were amazed at our first sight of the lavish gambling casino. It was obvious that millions had gone into its decor. At that time, there were only three hotels of any consequence: the Flamingo, the El Rancho Vegas, and the Last Frontier. The Flamingo was the first hotel and casino ever built in the desert of Nevada's Las Vegas. We had to gear our act to the gambling crowd and time it exactly so there was enough time for gambling. After all, that was the reason people came from all over the world—to gamble and be entertained. Performers received their highest salaries in Vegas. Little did we know that our boss was Bugsy Siegel, the notorious gangster, who later was assassinated by his own cohorts.

One of the owner-managers of the club took a special liking to us and invited us to his private dining room for lunch. He knew this was our first experience in Vegas, and he didn't want us to lose our salaries gambling. He kept warning us we couldn't win and expounded on his proven psychology of human nature. He told us it was rare for winners to hop the next plane home with their winnings, that in most cases they gave it all back and then some. He knew how hard we worked every night and made us promise to stay away from the tables.

Our wives were so fascinated by it all that they were tempted to become shills for the club. Fearing that they might become addicted, we quickly talked them out of it. To this day, Jessie can't forgive me for spoiling her fun. She was completely enamored by the dice tables. When payday arrived we made our way to our friend's office and asked him if he could cash our check so we could divide it three ways. He looked at us quizzically, smiled, and said, "Follow me, kids."

We followed him into a guarded room. We looked around and saw a group of men counting stacks of thousands of dollars in silver and currency. All I could think of saying was "Oh my God what a sight!" I realized that there was easily a million dollars in cash before our very eyes. It was mind-boggling to see so much money. Normally, no one was allowed into the counting room, but our boss knew whereof we came, and it obviously gave him extreme pleasure to shock our naive senses.

After seeing living proof as to where everyone's money ended up, we were convinced to stay away from the tables. Yet, even with all the warnings and all that we had seen, it was still fun dropping coins into the colorful one-armed bandits—just to see if we could win the jackpot. To know the truth was to spoil the fun. So we gave ourselves a very small allowance which we then handed over to our spouses to lose and enjoy.

Applaudience: The Autobiography of Dale Lind

Maestro Tommy Tucker (L) brings his popular recording orchestra to the screen in the new Universal-International musical featurette. Tucker is shown at left directing his orchestra and entertainers in a musical number, 1947

With all that time on their hands they had to do *something*. When I thought of how I had asked our boss if he could cash our puny check, it made me feel ridiculous.

One thing the bosses did not do was discourage gambling by actors and performers who came in from Hollywood. They were successful stars who made tons of money. They needed the excitement no matter what the cost. While the bosses smiled, the famous contributed. It was awesome to see so many movie stars, night after night. We became backstage buddies with Joey Bishop, who later joined Sinatra's Rat Pack, Shecky Greene, Jack E. Leonard, Alan King, and many others.

Star Billing in Vegas, A Fantasy Fulfilled

Lind Brothers play the Flamingo Hotel

There was no way we could ever have imagined what Vegas would become in the ensuing years. But we had the satisfaction of knowing that we were there at the beginning. We were asked to return again and again to play the El Rancho Vegas and the Last Frontier, where we headlined along with Martha Raye, Edgar Bergen, and the Rat Pack.

Vegas wasn't just work, work, work. There were many creature comforts provided for everyone. Sipping iced fruit drinks at the pool while the desert sun tanned our bodies was a refreshing delight. But my beloved, three months pregnant with our first child, could not fully enjoy our lavish surroundings. Jessie had constant attacks of nausea and was *losing* weight instead of gaining. I worried a great deal. In fact, since our marriage, it seemed like I could never let her suffer anything by herself. She had become such a part of me that I could sense when illness or pain was imminent, even before *she* knew about it. I had heard about people who thought alike, sensing each other's feelings and even predicting each other's actions, especially after many years of marriage.

As far as we were concerned, we were still like newlyweds, considering the war years of separation. In San Francisco, where we were appearing in the Bal Tabarin Room, I had symptoms *before* Jessie did. I had just reached our hotel room after a rehearsal when I felt nauseous. When I started throwing up in the bathroom, Jessie caught the mood and followed suit. I thought she was being empathetic, until she kept it up for two days. When the doctor confirmed our suspicions, we roared with laughter for days about my early symptoms. I never knew pregnancy could be so awful. Every time Jessie moaned, I groaned. I felt as if *I* was having the baby.

Before our Vegas engagement was half over, Jessie had a terrible attack of gagging and hiccupping. When I returned home after the last show, I found my sister-in-law, Rose, and the doctor, with Jessie. He told me she was dehydrating and rushed her to the hospital. They began to feed her intravenously immediately. When I noticed how green she was and the deep black bags under her eyes I got stomach cramps, and the doctor had to give *me* emergency treatment! Afterwards, he sat me down and said, "Look, she'd be better off at home, under more normal circumstances. If I were you, I'd send her home as soon as possible. In fact, you'll both be better off."

As long as I've known Jessie, she was never that sick. Actually, the baby was too large for her to carry, especially as it laid lopsided in her body. Watching her suffer made me realize even more how much I loved her. She was my very heartbeat! If I could have taken over her suffering, I would have done it gladly.

In my dressing room before showtime, my brothers tried to calm me down, but nothing was working. I was too stressed out. I thought, "God, if she loses the baby, she'll be even sicker." As disciplined and controlled as I was in my work, the worry was breaking me down completely. I could hardly get into my show clothes. I felt like I was losing it. Murray and Phil finally broke my mood by saying, "Dale, you have to buck up, there's a crowd out there waiting to hear us. You know, the show must go on. Jessie would want you to, no matter what." I knew they were right, and I couldn't let them down. After all, we were the Three Musketeers: all for one, and one for all. That was our creed! I pulled myself up from the couch, straightened up and quickened my step to the stage. As our music started, the emcee introduced us with, "Here they are, ladies and gentlemen, The Three Lind Brothers!" Applause broke out as we ran to the microphone and started singing our opening number, "Camptown Races." From there on in, I felt fine.

In between shows, I rushed to the hospital to be with Jess, and perked her up as best I could. Of course, our kisses and hugs helped a lot—for both of us. At night I couldn't sleep. I realized the doctor was right about sending her home, but I hated the thought of traveling without her. My successes wouldn't feel the same. I needed her close to me, for inspiration, for comfort, for love…but her health was certainly more important than my personal feelings. I knew her mother would really pamper her, and Jessie was due for a little spoiling. She needed rest, care, and her mom's fabulous home-cooked meals.

Jessie's mother was a power-house! Fanny could do anything. By noon every day her house was cleaned and immaculate. At 6:00 A.M., dinner was being prepared for her Jake and their three sons, Fran, Robert, and Irving. She spent hours in the morning doing all her chores so she could devote the rest of her time to synagogue and charitable activities. Mom was a marvelous soul. When she knew I was coming to Elmira for a visit, she would prepare all my favorite dishes. Fanny was known as a kosher-gourmet, and Diamond Jim couldn't have fared better. I was fortunate to have the kind of in-laws I had. They gave me respect and love and I returned it in kind. I knew that Jess would be surrounded by family and friends who adored her, and that helped me to finally make up my mind. As soon as it was feasible, Jessie returned to Elmira, where she was welcomed by all the family. It brought me great comfort to know she was in good hands.

Chapter 29

REUNIONS & A NEWCOMER

Our Vegas engagement had ended, and it was time for us, with regret, to move on to other challenges. Such is the life for performers—travel and more travel. I wasn't happy leaving Vegas. Performing in all three hotels as headliners had been an exciting and satisfying experience.

Our next booking was at the Ambassador Hotel in Los Angeles. It was a prestigious room and drew a terrific crowd, including movie stars. The surprise of that engagement was when Danny Thomas showed up with his whole family. We hadn't seen him since the Philippines. Seeing him as a husband and father was so different. There were no jokes. He didn't have to entertain us. He was there to enjoy us as colleagues. He told us that he wanted to expose his children to "clean entertainment—no scantily-clad chorus girls and no obscene comics." We appreciated that.

Sitting with him at his table, I couldn't help noticing his little girl, Marlo. She was so cute. I could never have imagined her so grown up later, as the star of her own television show, "That Girl." Why was I surprised? She was following in her father's footsteps. Today, she continues to be the spokeswoman for St. Jude's Children's Hospital, which Danny helped build and support, raising millions of dollars to help cure children from around the globe, at no charge. There is a story about Danny and St. Jude. When Danny was desperately trying to make good in Hollywood, he turned to St. Jude, his patron saint, and prayed for help. His faith in St. Jude was so strong, that he made him a promise: that he would dedicate his life to helping build a multi-million dollar facility for research and cures for children's illnesses. Obviously, his prayers were answered, and Danny kept his promise until the day he died.

Applaudience: The Autobiography of Dale Lind

The three Lind brothers as entertainers, 1950's

Danny was not only a wonderful comedian and actor, but also an astute business man. He and his partner, Sheldon Leonard, knew that television, though in its infancy, was the place to be. Together, they produced shows like "Make Room for Daddy," in which Danny starred. It became their first smash serial hit. Danny also starred in the movie, "The Jazz Singer," the life of Al Jolson. He made other movies, as well, which established him as one of the great performers of our time. In Los Angeles, we reminisced about the past with Danny and enjoyed our reunion.

In December of 1948, we made our way back from the West Coast to the Chase Hotel in St. Louis. Jessie was in her ninth month! As soon as our engagement was over, I left for Elmira to be with her, hoping to welcome our first child together. No luck! We were slated to open at the

Nicollet Hotel in Minneapolis on January 2. I had no choice, so I left Elmira on New Year's Day. When I arrived at the hotel in Minneapolis, the clerk handed me a telegram from my brother-in-law Bob, in Elmira, congratulating me on becoming a father! I let out a hoot and a holler in the lobby, and my brothers joined me in celebrating my first-born. Jessie and I had decided if we had a son, we would name him Cary Alan. "Cary" was "*Chayim*" in Hebrew, which meant "life." He would have a good, long one, we hoped.

During our Minneapolis engagement, I was concerned and anxious because we had six weeks of bookings ahead of us before I could even think of returning home to Jessie and our first-born. Sadly, I wouldn't be there for Cary's circumcision. I felt antsy and guilty, but I couldn't leave our act in the lurch. After Minneapolis, we were booked into Milwaukee for four weeks. I asked Shelley not to book us after that, so I could spend some time with Jessie and our son. During those long weeks, I found comfort in the fact that Cary had ten fingers and toes, that he and Jessie were both well, and that I could look forward to being with them for the rest of my life.

It was strange that when the Minneapolis theatre pages announced our engagement at the Nicollet, the majority of our audiences were Swedish. The name "Lind" lulled them into thinking we were Swedish, and they turned out en masse. On opening night, after a wonderful reception, we were asked by many present to sing something Swedish. The next day we ran to a music store and found what became a permanent song in our international repertoire, "Ya Sure, You Betcha, You Betcha Ay Do." We learned some Swedish steps from one of the dancers on the bill, bought some Swedish hats with feathers, and presented the song nightly. The Swedish crowds loved it, and when our engagement was over, the management assured us we would return in the near future.

On the plane back to Elmira, I felt like I was having an anxiety attack. One of the stewardesses calmed me down by serving me tea and cookies. She kept conversing with me, which I appreciated, as it relaxed me. I

Applaudience: The Autobiography of Dale Lind

Lind Brothers singing their famous Swedish favorite "Ya Sure You Betcha" in Minneapolis at the Nicollet Hotel, 1949

closed my eyes so I could sleep a while. I was tired, having done two shows the night before. But I was stimulated about being with Jess and our baby. I slept for the rest of our flight and awoke hours later, when the announcement came over the speakers to fasten our seatbelts.

As we descended to the runway, my heart beat a mile a minute. When the plane landed, I rushed to the exit and flew down the steps. My brother-in-law, Bob, was waiting to pick me up and drive me to our home. When we reached our house on Washington Street, the family was waiting for me, some outside and the rest inside.

Before I knew it, Jessie was in my arms. I hugged her so tightly that she said, "Ow." We smothered each other with kisses. As I looked to my side, there was my wonderful mother-in-law and father-in-law, Fanny and Jake, holding Cary. Tears streaked down my face as I saw Cary for the first time. I was bursting with emotion, and I could hardly contain myself.

I took him in my arms and raised him up as high as I could. He giggled and screamed, and I burst into laughter. For me, it was a supreme moment! Ah, but then came a surprise. As I held him on my shoulder, he threw up all over my brand new suit. Jessie hadn't warned me about him being a spitter. I didn't care. Nothing was as important as holding my son in my arms. His hair was blond and he was fair-skinned, like me. He had our family features. It felt good to know that he would carry on the family name. I was proud of that, and thankful that God had blessed us with our first child.

As the months went on, it got harder to leave them again and again, but Shelley kept booking us into eastern clubs like Buffalo's, New York's "Town Casino," Montreal's "Normandy Roof," and other prestigious show places. This gave us the opportunity to see each other more often. Some months later, Jessie began traveling with me again. This time, however, we had a third passenger, Cary, with his crib and all the rest of the paraphernalia. We were lucky—he was a good baby. He ate and slept well, was rarely crabby, and was a wonderful child to be with. I knew that he had the same genes as Jessie—cool and calm, and that was a lot better than my fiery temperament.

As the years went on, Cary proved his coolness under fire, as he sailed through life calmly in every circumstance.

Chapter 30

Ups & Downs In Paradise

Phil Shelley brought us great news. He had finally succeeded in getting our first Miami Beach engagement, at the Schyler brothers' Five O'clock Club. Those were the days when Miami hotels were restricted from operating nightclubs on their premises. Therefore, the private clubs were flourishing, and The Five was one of the most successful. It was located on Collins Avenue, the main stem of Miami Beach, which ran from the lowest end of the beach to the northern tip and contained miles and miles of many-splendored hotels.

We arrived in Miami by plane at night. I thought we were entering Paradise as we gaped at thousands of colored lights, all designed to outline the magnificent hotel skyline. The greatest designers in the world had been hired as hotels tried to outdo each other. Because of the lights, a heavenly halo emanated from the structures, extending high above the rooftops. We were dumbstruck by its beauty.

The carefree atmosphere of resort life was obvious as soon as we landed at the airport. Thousands of tanned Miamians were meeting relatives and friends, all in their colorful sportswear. We knew that Florida would be a totally different experience than Vegas. It would be "fun in the sun" with no gambling but with much to enjoy. When we reached our hotel we quickly checked in and immediately went *shpatziring*, roaming, in and out of different hotel lobbies all designed in a royal manner. We didn't know it, but we were doing exactly what all newcomers do—appraising the plush surroundings. We heard patrons saying quietly:

"Golda, this carpeting must cost $10,000."

"And look at those purple drapes, at least $25,000."

We began to feel Miami Beach would be the most exciting place we had ever known. We set out newly inspired to make our debut a triumph.

Our Chicago following really paid off, as they packed the club nightly. We made a real dent in Miami night life. We appeared on The Barry Gray Radio Talk Show and various other programs. The Schuyler Brothers, owners of the Five O'Clock Club, thought we were a phenomenon for a relatively unknown Miami act.

But it was after the shows that we used to get the special kicks that only performers in their own crazy world can truly appreciate. Night after night, after our midnight shows, we met with other performers to unwind at Wolfie's restaurant on Collins Avenue. Lenny Kent, our co-star, along with Jackie Miles and Harvey Stone, would let their hair down, and their hilarious and *haimishe*—warm, homey—stories would last till the wee hours of the morning.

The Schuyler brothers, along with other partners, also owned one of the largest nightclubs in Miami. Consequently, we were booked into their Copa City directly from the Five O'clock Club, which was an important step up. It was a big show with big names, and Joe E. Lewis headlined the bill. We were now batting in the big leagues.

The Beachcomber, directly across the street, featured the great new comedy team of Martin and Lewis. Jerry's father, Danny Lewis, had sung in the Borscht Belt in the Catskills for many years while Jerry was growing up. Because Danny loved singing, he was in our audience almost nightly, and we got to know each other well. He must have told Jerry about us because one night there he was, catching our act. When we repaid the visit the very same night, Jerry began mimicking our act as soon as he spotted us. The audience howled at his antics and we were glad to be the victims. This was as great a compliment as any star could pay another act.

Miamians accepted us and opened their hearts and homes, and we were delighted with our new friends. Our days and nights were filled with exciting times, and Jessie and I wished we could live in Florida forever. Our friends, the Hertz family, invited us to join them on their boat. They served food and drinks and taught us how to troll. What a wonderful way to spend a day in the Florida Bay.

One night at Copa City, one of the owners walked up to us and said, "Look, I don't want you guys to sing any religious numbers tonight." He had a big, ugly scar on his face and looked like he was from Murder, Inc. We knew he was referring to *"Eili Eili,"* a Jewish lament to God, and *"Ave Maria."* I took a strong stand and answered back, "No way, we can't cut out our show stoppers. We're associated with those songs, and our audiences wait for them."

Then I saw his eyes fill with venom and I backed away as he sneered, "If you know what's good for you, you'll do as I say or it's your asses...." He looked so vicious that my brothers and I were really frightened. We couldn't understand his sudden change of attitude.

We decided to talk to Ned Schuyler immediately. We cornered him and told him what had happened, and Ned said, "Look, kids, I love your act just the way it is, but I can't get involved in a fight with my partners over this. If you feel that you must sing those songs, sing 'em, but leave me out of it."

It was like an Abbott and Costello routine: one said, "Don't," while the other said, "Do." We talked it over in our dressing room and decided reluctantly to cut the numbers out of our show. As we stood backstage waiting for our emcee's introduction, we overheard one of the performers say, "Do you know who's out there tonight?"

Another answered, "Yeah. Meyer Lansky, Sam Giancana, and other Mafia guys." We asked them where they were sitting. "Right out front, with their diamond-studded ladies." Now we knew why Scarface didn't want us to sing any religious songs. He probably felt his guests would feel uncomfortable. After all, they represented the *Mafia*.

As we went into our act, we saw Scarface on one side of the stage, watching, listening, and waiting for the conclusion of our performance. Now we began to think all kinds of things. We had heard that "the boys" controlled many of the clubs around the country, and for the first time in our career we felt threatened.

I couldn't fathom Scarface's sudden antagonism toward religious songs. He had heard and seen our standing ovations night after night as we closed with *"Eili Eili"* on one show and *"Ave Maria"* on the next. He had been present, too, when the incomparable Sophie Tucker celebrated her birthday at the Copa City one night after the last show and insisted that we sing *"Eili Eili."*

We finished our act with *"Vesti La Giubba"* from the opera, Pagliacci, and walked off to a tremendous ovation. Scarface stared at us coldly. As we returned to take our bows, the audience began to yell *"Eili Eili, Ave Maria, Eili Eili."* As they kept it up, the orchestra conductor looked at us, waiting for our cue.

My brothers and I just looked at each other, and having worked together for so many years, we knew we were all thinking the same thing. At that moment, with the audience clamoring for our most poignant songs, we had no alternative but to oblige. We were idealistic enough to believe that it was our duty as artists to give of ourselves completely. We could never feel fulfilled as performers if we did not perform to the very best of our ability. That was our credo throughout our career.

As we finished *"Eili Eili"* with the lines, "Let My People Go," the audience stood up, cheering. So did "the boys"—no matter what Meyer Lansky represented, he was still Jewish, and when he heard us sing, "Let my people go," he joined the ovation. His cohorts followed suit and joined the crowd. It was a triumph for us, but not for Scarface, who was used to being obeyed. Under my breath, I mumbled to my brothers to exit from the other side. I wanted to avoid looking at Scarface again. I had remembered that when Joe E. Lewis was a young performer, he was beat up by hoods and left for dead in a Chicago alley because he had switched to another club that was competing for his services, after having been warned not to do it.

We took a last bow and ran to our dressing room. We jumped into our street clothes without taking time to remove our make-up. We vamoosed—and quickly! I didn't sleep well that night. I remembered that Lewis' tongue had been cut mercilessly! The next day we found a message at the desk to call Schuyler at Copa City. I had a premonition that we were being sacked by Scarface. There was no way the Schuylers could win our case. We disobeyed the boss and never really knew who he was. Obviously, he had the power to do as he wished.

When Schuyler told us we would have to leave Copa City, we were very upset. Years later, we were informed that we were lucky to be alive. Scarface was one of the higher-up's—in other words, the Cosa Nostra. The Schyler Brothers had spoken on our behalf, saying that we were kids, that we didn't know any better, that we were insignificant, and it would not serve them well to hurt us. To this day, Scarface's real name is unknown to me.

From what we were told, the Schuylers spoke to Lansky, who had the power to dissuade Scarface from doing us any harm. Fate again was on our side, that Lansky was there that night at Copa City. Otherwise, God knows what would have happened to us! As for Scarface, he didn't have our asses as he vowed—they're still in tact to this day.

It's interesting to note that, years later, Lansky's Jewishness became more important to him. While under investigation by the criminal justice system, he escaped to Israel with his millions, hoping to live there for the rest of his life. But Israel wanted no such citizen and extradited him back to the USA. Besides, he was under indictment, and the Israeli government wanted no part of protecting a member of the Mafia.

After firing us from Copa City, Schuyler rebooked us immediately into The Five O'Clock Club, as co-stars with Jackie Miles. We were relieved and happy because we loved The Five. It was intimate and warm, a performer's favorite kind of room. After three fabulous months among the palm trees, our honeymoon with Miami came to an end. We hated to leave. It was a glorious chapter that we hoped to relive some day . . . but without Scarface!

Chapter 31

STRANGE DESTINY

Shelley was determined to book us into New York's world-famous Copacabana. He felt that such a booking would enhance our careers and catapult us to the top. But Fate decreed otherwise. While flying to New York, Shelley became deathly ill. He had had very little sleep prior to his trip and felt miserable. The stewardesses did their best to make him comfortable, but it was all to no avail. When his plane landed at La Guardia, Phil began throwing up. A short time later, while in a cab on his way from the airport, he developed pains in his arms and legs. By the time he reached The Copa, the pain had reached his heart. He emerged from the cab in agony and fell to the ground, dying instantly from a massive coronary.

When the news reached us, we went into shock. This just couldn't be—it seemed impossible. Phil was always so strong and impregnable. We just couldn't accept it. Later, when the reality of it finally came into focus, we were almost panicky! He had been the captain of our ship and had steered our destiny so successfully. He was more than our manager, he was our friend, our defender and champion. This was a wound that would not heal quickly, if it healed at all. It was really a time for mourning. We were all deeply troubled, and frightened that somehow our careers would never be the same again with Shelley gone.

After some weeks had passed, we realized that we needed a new captain if we were to survive in the jungle of show business. We remembered a very successful New York lawyer who had served in the Army with us and who had always professed a strong interest in our act. When we walked into his plush offices, Jonas Silverstone threw his arms

Applaudience: The Autobiography of Dale Lind

Lind Brothers staring at New York's Broadway Strand Theatre, 1947

around us. He quickly ushered us into the office of his partner, Mort Rosenthal, recalling some of the typical Army miseries we had mutually suffered. Now we could laugh about them. Jonas said, "Okay, fellas, get to work. There will be no loitering here. Clean up the kitchen, the latrine, and then report back for guard duty tonight!"

"Yes, Sir!" we said, saluting, and then burst into screaming laughter. Mort got some coffee and danish pastry for us, as we reminisced a bit more. We felt at home with them.

We must have been in conference for two hours discussing our accomplishments and our dreams for the future. During the conversation we discovered that Jonas and Mort were now representing Victor Borge and the Ink Spots, two phenomenal acts. They were also the legal office for the American Guild of Variety Artists and the Actors' Union. We decided to put our fate in their hands. Jonas and Mort weren't agents; they would act in the capacity of business lawyers representing our best interests. As soon as we signed with them, they contacted The William Morris Agency about booking us. They also contacted super agents who had the power to secure prime engagements. Our past successes helped them give us a strong entrée into the best theatres and clubs.

This was quite different from the way our one-man dynamo had worked; Shelley had done everything himself. He had cajoled nightclub owners until they came to terms. He wheeled and dealed and persisted as a man obsessed with breaking down every barrier so his acts could get a shot at the best in show business. Jonas gradually turned us over to Mort, the younger partner, and a shrewd representative. We became good friends, and began to feel more confident with our new management as important bookings developed. Our first date was at the Broadway Strand Theatre in New York City, an outstanding movie and Vaudeville house. We were to co-star with comedy star Billy Vine and violinist Florian Zabach and his orchestra.

The thrill of seeing our name in lights on a Broadway marquee defies description. It was something we had dreamed about ever since we had begun as a trio some six years before. We walked outside between shows and just stared at the marquee from across the street. When we walked on stage for our first show, well—we never actually walked, we usually ran to center stage! The theatre was jammed for our first performance, and I could feel Phil shaking next to me. I didn't dare say anything to make him more aware of his nervousness. We knew the critics were there, too, as well as our new managers. We opened our show with the lightning "Sabre Dance," and followed with a pop song of the day. Then the stage went dark and we began the poignant *"Ave Maria."* There was only one pin-spot on our faces, and the audience stopped breathing. When we concluded with "Amen," fading out ever so softly in falsetto harmony, a stunning ovation rang out. We knew we had won our greatest victory to date.

Our success at the Strand earned us a special bonus. The William Morris Agency booked us into the Chicago Theatre as an "Extra Added

Attraction" with movie star Alan Young. What a way for us to return home—appearing in Chicago's largest and most prestigious Vaudeville house. We were introduced to the opening act, a fellow called Liberace. Little did we know that he would become a superstar through television. For now, he had to be content to open the show, which he did amiably while winning ovation after ovation. He proved his talent as a master showman, show after show.

We invited our Mom and Dad to come backstage before our first show. Before entering, they stopped to look at the marquee. When they saw our names in blazing lights, they shed tears. They entered the theatre and the doorman led them to our dressing room. They hugged and kissed us and congratulated us on reaching a milestone in our career. Then Dad donned his yarmulke, raised his hands over our heads, and blessed us with the three-fold blessing of all faiths, which begins with the words, "May the Lord bless you and keep you." Tears welled up in our eyes as he finished with, "May the Lord grant you peace." It touched our hearts and we knew that we were the luckiest guys in the world to hear such deep caring words from our father. Our mother stood there in awe of everything that was happening. Then we got the "ten minute" call for our turn on stage.

As we led our folks into the theatre from the backstage door, we could hear the musicians taking their places on stage. It was important for the orchestra to begin their theme at the precise moment the movie screen disappeared and the curtain started to open. As our conductor, Lou Breese, a commanding figure in his formal dress, gave the signal with his baton, the timpani roared and the horns blared, filling the theatre with a glorious introduction to our stage show.

The regimen of Vaudeville was a true test of stamina, as we had to perform five and six shows a day, every day. The discipline of winning an audience in ten to twelve minutes was always a challenge, and every act on the bill had to observe the discipline of timing their routines exactly. After our first show at The Chicago Theatre, all the acts were summoned to Abe Platt's conference room above the theatre. He was in charge of

Strange Destiny

Lind Brothers starring at Chicago's Oriental Theatre, 1947

everything that took place in the theatre, the screen and vaudeville presentations as well as the timing schedules. As the general manager, Platt answered only to his bosses, Balaban and Katz, and what he said to all of us as we sat there, a bit tense, was absolute law.

No one dared question his authority when he said things like, "You were on too long. I want you to cut this and do only that." And so it went with Liberace, the Lind Brothers, Alan Young, and others. In the end, we had a tightly knit show which proved to be a winner, and we were held over again and again, with thousands of people and critics acclaiming our success. We sang for 15,000 people a day, making a total of over 400,000 during our four-week engagement.

Doing so many shows each day meant spending most of our time backstage. As a result, the acts became like one big happy family, especially during longer engagements. Bridge, gin rummy, and poker were the games of the day. The girls in the show constantly worked on their costumes, sewing and repairing while they created new ways to improve their acts. The whole atmosphere was vibrant with activity. I loved the smell of the greasepaint, hearing the musicians tuning up and the singers vocalizing, watching acrobats limbering up in their colorful costumes, the sparkle and glitter of dance teams tapping away, effervescent and happy in their dream world of excitement and glamour. Our show broke all attendance records, and as a result we gained a return engagement at Chicago's Oriental Theatre as the sole headliners, which gave us the stature we needed to progress in show business.

Some time later, we read in *Variety* about a club which was red-hot, "The Vine Gardens," on Chicago's North Avenue. Jimmy Pappas, its owner, contacted our managers and offered us a four week contract. We would be following a newcomer by the name of Joey Bishop, who was hailed as a rising comedy star. He was destined to become a member of "the Rat Pack," with Frank Sinatra, Dean Martin, Sammy Davis, Jr. and Peter Lawford.

The nightclub scene was vastly different from theatre because audiences smoked, ate, and drank during performances. Inhaling the stink of smoke-filled vapors made singing very difficult. Still, we had no alternative but to grin and bear it. During our nightclub engagements we ate breakfast at 1:00 A.M., retired at 3:00 A.M., and slept till noon. Jessie and I would go to the movies in the afternoon or shop. We ate dinner early so I could ready myself for three shows every night. I always enjoyed the frivolity and excitement as we prepared ourselves backstage, applying our make-up, checking our clothes, and vocalizing. All of us felt that special emotional rush that only Applaudiences can bring to performers. The drama of it all was so stimulating that I still long for the anticipation of appearing in a spotlight on stage.

Money was rolling in, and everything seemed to be going right. At the same time, however, Senator Estes Kefauver began closing down nightclub operations that featured gambling in the back rooms. It did not affect us at the Vine, as they had no gambling, and our booking there turned out to be the longest of our careers. We did SRO business for six solid months, and Pappas proudly displayed the new kitchen our profits had brought in. When our engagement there ended, everyone at the Vine, including us, was sad. We felt like we were leaving home. Then, suddenly, we lost sixteen weeks of bookings as club owners began canceling all higher-priced acts. Without gambling, clubs all over the country were doomed. Many owners found themselves unable to meet the inflated salaries of their favorite stars, which included us. We sensed that night clubs, as we knew them, were on the way to extinction, except for Vegas and other locations where gambling was legal.

After two months of idleness, we appeared on national television when the "Show of Shows" was based in Chicago. Our sketch was about a typical New York gathering on the East Side, with immigrants in their native garb and the local cop on the beat. It gave us the opportunity to sing our *"Eili Eili"* for a national audience. We received accolades from listeners around the country, but somehow we still felt insecure and worried about the future. Mort sensed our despair and frustration and flew to Chicago to have a serious discussion with us. He had been able to get a commitment for us to appear at Alan Gale's club in Miami for six months. Conditions, however, were not good, and we could not afford to work for the low salary we were being offered. With three of us and our families to support, the costs of our business managers, new musical arrangements, and a myriad of other continuing expenses, we had a lot to think about. Our entire future was now at stake!

We weighed our decision for days. We were tired of traveling and feeling like gypsies. Our children would be of school age. We longed for a more stable life, with permanent roots. Chicago was our natural choice, the place where we had been the most successful and where our parents lived. Reluctantly, we notified Mort that we were quitting, while still wondering if we were making the right decision. Mort did not have the persuasive powers of a Phil Shelley and could not change our minds. It was a decision we would think about for the rest of our lives.

When the Andrews Sisters broke up, we couldn't believe it. How was it possible for one of the greatest and most successful teams in show business? But it happened! And when Patti Andrews went on alone, it was never the same. Then other break-ups followed: the Williams Brothers, the Ames Brothers, and the McGuire Sisters. Later, the greatest comedy team of all, Martin and Lewis, went their separate ways, as well. Everyone thought Dean Martin would go down the tubes while Jerry Lewis would fly high. They were wrong. Both of them made it big, REAL BIG!

It's unfortunate that acts break up. I thought it would never happen to *us,* but it did! I never dreamed that in future years, I would become an entrepreneur, a party consultant, a restaurant and club owner, and also resume my role as a cantor and clergyman. Who can possibly foresee what the future holds in store for anyone?

As the months and years passed, I often thought about our decision. So many of our pals in show business gained national fame through the magic of television and through movies, which were bigger than ever. Some years later, I walked up to Alan King when he appeared at the Nippersink Resort in Wisconsin. When he saw me, he said, "Oh my God. Where have you guys been? Do you realize you could be making $25,000 for guest shots on television?" It was like a shot to my solar plexus. I just smiled, because I really had no answer.

Alan King, Jan Murray, Liberace, Alan Young, Jack Carter, and so many others who stayed in show business, really made it in a big way. As time passed, I kept thinking of Shelley. Had he lived, he probably would have changed the course of our lives, for he was the master puppeteer and we were his favorite three puppets. He used to say to Jessie, "If for some reason I can't keep the boys together, then at least let me have Dale as a single." But God knew otherwise, for Shelley, who wanted so much to live, was long gone. There is an old saying among my people: *"Der mench tracht, un Gott lacht!"* "Man plans, while God laughs!"

Chapter 32

THE BIRTH OF ISRAEL

It was 1948, the year that Jews around the world will never forget. There was passionate rejoicing by Jews everywhere as President Truman recognized our new State of Israel. For over two thousand years Jews had wandered from place to place looking for a homeland where their families could be safe from anti-Semitism. Even in America, there was still the feeling of rejection, as prejudice constantly reared its ugly head in almost every facet of life.

With Israel now a reality, oppressed Jews from the whole planet could migrate to their Promised Land. I couldn't help thinking of the six million martyrs whose bodies were exhumed in the crematoria of Hitler's concentration camps. If only there had been an Israel to run to then, but destiny had ruled otherwise. Now, Israel was a reality, an outgrowth of the pogroms and indignities that our ancestors had suffered for generations.

I would like to think that the millions of souls of our martyred brothers and sisters had cried out from the heavens for justice and mercy—that God Himself finally intervened through dedicated leaders like Theodore Hertzl, Chaim Weitzman, and David Ben Gurion, who brought our dream to fruition.

The struggle for recognition had been heroic but costly, as Israelis shed blood and tears and gave their lives for their homeland in five bloody wars. When word of their great resistance reached the ears of Chicago Jewry, a champion rose up to volunteer his services to command an official U.S. Jewish army of volunteers. But Washington would not hear of it. They forbade our great ex-marine friend, Barney Ross, from continuing his quest. Thousands of ex-servicemen throughout America had volunteered including my brothers and me, but Pentagon approval never came.

So we moved in other directions, calling secret meetings to raise arms and ammunition for Hagganah (the Israeli Army) by every possible means. We knew that they spelled the difference between life and death. We were proud there were outstanding men like Colonel Mickey Marcus who successfully made their way to Israel to join the fight.

Our entire beings shook with intense anxiety as Israel fought for independence. Their victory would be our victory, or their destruction, God forbid; we couldn't even think of that kind of result. To think that some day I, too, could pray at the "Wailing Wall" was more than I could bear. For hadn't we always concluded the *Neelah* service at the end of *Yom Kippur*, our holiest day of the year, with the prophetic words *"Leshana Haba Birusholayim,"* "Next year in Jerusalem"?

As Israel became a reality, money was sorely needed, so we made our trio available to the Israel Bond office for appearances anywhere and everywhere. Before long we were provided with a private plane to fly us throughout the country, wherever our services were needed and requested. We sang and cajoled every Jew we came in contact with to empty their pockets, assuring them it was not only a good dollar investment, but an even more important investment in the future of all Jewry, in every part of the world.

All of us genuinely believed that a strong and creative Israel would bring new understanding and respect for our people and our heritage. Bond drives were set up in Chicago's City Hall and on the open streets, with bandstands, microphones and lecterns, as thousands of Jews gathered to help Israel. Many stripped themselves of every penny they possessed and bought bonds. Others went into hock as they borrowed for our Holy Land. The Lind Brothers had suddenly become a symbol for our great common cause—and no one could refuse our appeal as we sold songs for Bond Dollars.

We felt caught up in a wave of Idealism and Purpose to sustain what so many worked to accomplish. The toughest ones to sell were those who denied their Jewishness and wanted no part of the new State. Fortunately, we succeeded in selling Israeli bonds amounting to millions of dollars. Never had we known such elation and satisfaction in our work. We had reaped great sums of money for a cause dear to our hearts and our people.

We enjoyed one of our greatest thrills while conducting a parlor meeting prior to a large bond dinner at the Nicollet Hotel in Minneapolis. While we were performing, there was suddenly a great commotion. Then applause broke out as our bond representative excitedly walked in with Senator John Kennedy. The Kennedy name was so famous and glamorous that I never expected to meet such a humble, gentle man. As he shook my hand and looked at me from deep-set, blue, penetrating eyes, I could not imagine that his name would someday become immortal! Now I always feel that I have attained a link with eternity.

The bond appearances were the crowning achievement to our retirement from show business. How could we ever evaluate what we had accomplished? I don't know if we could have dedicated ourselves so deeply if we had continued in show business. Perhaps I am trying to convince myself that it was all *bashert*, or predestined. I have always been a believer in Fate, and certainly the cause for Israel could compensate somewhat for the inner conflict and frustrations I have had to bear. True, I had hated certain aspects of the show business we knew. Days and weeks could be so tedious and lonely, especially when we were separated from loved ones as we traveled endlessly. Still, the love and inner satisfaction I felt each time we stood on stage was equally true. When I picked up newspapers from different cities and saw "The Lind Brothers" in theatre ads, and blazing in big lights on marquees, I was ready to burst with that special glow of fulfillment. It was a dream come true!

Only the future could tell me if I could bear the choice we had made. I prayed to the Almighty that I would not be plagued by the glowing memories we had with so many talented people we had come to know and love. Already I missed them terribly, especially the camaraderie we enjoyed. When the comics got together, their stories were hilarious! I remember sitting with Henny Youngman in New York in Lindy's Restaurant. He spoke of a patient who was getting a check-up from his doctor. After examining him, the doctor gave him six months to live. When the patient replied, "But Doctor, I won't be able to pay your bill," the Doctor answered, "So I'll give you another six months." Henny went on and said, "My mother-in-law came to visit me recently and I said to her, 'Ma, I want you to be happy here. Just make my house your house'…so she sold it!"

I miss Henny, and others like Chicago's Jackie Leonard, who was a very funny guy and a good friend. My life will never be the same. One thing I *do* know. I'll never stop singing. It's my life's blood. Nothing can change that. I've always known that I was born to sing. My life is proof of that, and I will continue to sing until my dying hour…and if I can't sing, I'll hum.

Chapter 33

WHO SAID IT IS BETTER TO VENTURE & LOSE?

We had been through so much as a team that we decided to sink or swim together. We agreed to invest all our savings in a retail business. We created and opened the first ultra-glamorous boy's store in the entire country. Catering to boys only, it had a sports department, shoe department, toy department, barber shop, and even a kiddie-land. It was a boy's heaven, so we named it "Boys' World."

Our first Boys' World store was on the south side of Chicago in the Beverly section. We were so successful that within two years we opened a second and larger store on the North Side's Devon Avenue. For that opening, we contacted Andy Devine and Guy Madison to parade down Devon Avenue in their Western garb. Thousands of people lined the streets, thrilled to see the two famous stars cut the ribbon, officially opening our store. Hordes of people and boys swarmed into the plush surroundings. It was a fantastic opening day, and the cash registers jingled continuously. As the months went on we began to feel that maybe we *had* made the right decision after all.

It was on a July fourth week-end, when we were all relaxing and enjoying the holiday, disturbed only by intermittent sounds of popping fire-crackers when we received an urgent call from the police. The biggest fire-cracker of them all had just exploded in our Devon Avenue store. Spontaneous combustion had taken place through a combination of heat and loose wiring, and the devastating fire brought firemen from several districts. Our store was a total disaster and was completely gutted.

Lind Brothers opening Boy's World store in Chicago with screen stars Andy Devine and Guy Madison cutting the ribbon

Hundreds of thousands of dollars in merchandise and fixtures not yet fully paid for were reduced to ashes. We had taken our huge responsibility too lightly and had not insured ourselves properly. Consequently, it was a staggering financial loss and a severe blow to our retail career. The only thing we were able to salvage was our giant world globe that was outside on top of the store. We ended up selling it to Thillens Park on Devon Avenue. Repainted into a giant baseball, it now represents their baseball field.

Dejected, broke, and thoroughly depressed, we had no choice but to sell the Beverly store to satisfy the creditors. With all the *tzores* (troubles) that we were encountering, we were still determined to keep our good name and integrity by paying all our suppliers what we owed them. At a crucial time like that, I could only think of something Dad used to tell us: Do not tread in strange domains. It was Dad's philosophy that we are all born to do what we know best and would be better off not to stray into other fields. Although this was not true with everyone, it seemed to be deadly accurate with us. If only we had listened to Dad's prophetic words. But how many kids listen to their parents?

Someone once said, "It is better to venture and lose, than never to venture at all!" That is easier said than done, as we discovered too late. I still say that Boys' World, albeit a gutsy new idea, was a great success while it lasted . . . but who can fight the fates? Jessie and I had five great words we always used when catastrophes of any kind struck. These words always erased our pain and gave us new hope. When we lost Boys' World, we looked at each other and said, *"And this, too, shall pass."* And it did, eventually.

Once again we had to look to new horizons for our talents.

Chapter 34

My Kids—The Troupers

As the years went on, our trio fizzled. We had no alternative but to go our own ways professionally. Phil became a radio disc-jockey and also produced a local television show. Murray became a full-time cantor on Chicago's North Side, but was prohibited by his congregation from singing anywhere that smacked of show business. Although I, too, was cantoring on the South Side of Chicago, my synagogue was more liberal and was proud of my concertizing and entertaining. I was therefore able to join Phil on his television show, which was staged at the Civic Opera House. We sang solos and duets backed by the CBS Orchestra. The show lasted for many months and just for a while, Phil and I were back in show business together.

At the time, Jessie and I were living in Park Forest, a suburb far south of Chicago. Jessie and her brother, Fran, had become partners in a women's sportswear shop there, while our son was growing up. It wasn't easy for Jess to be running a shop when she became pregnant with our second child. Cary was already four and a half when Barbara came into our world. She was so cute, and we were so taken with our newborn, that all of us treated her like a princess…a Jewish one at that! All of Park Forest knew of Barb's birth. We got headlines in the local paper because Jessie wrote a weekly column that she called "Fran's Fripperies." She wrote about fashion and events in the community, and the local women loved it. Her column the week after July 16, 1952, was all about our new baby.

Once again, as with our son, we were elated. We felt lucky and happy to have two normal children. Life was good—so many things to look forward to with our kids. Cary was already showing musical ability, and I wondered if Barbara, too, would inherit some of my singing genes…

Applaudience: The Autobiography of Dale Lind

Dale and children Cary, 10 and Barbara, 7, in dress rehersal, 1958

When Barb reached the age of four, Cary had already been singing with me for several years, both in shows, entertaining, and at my synagogue as a soloist in the choir. As he strummed his ukelele while singing, Barb listened to him in awe. One day, as we were rehearsing for a show at the Nippersink Resort in Wisconsin, I heard a small voice singing and mumbling in the background. Looking around, I noticed Barbara singing along with us. I couldn't believe what I was hearing! She was only four and a half, and yet there she was, with her rosy fat cheeks and tiny rosebud mouth, singing our routines perfectly. For many months she had been listening and learning our routines during our rehearsals. I looked at her standing there, so tiny in her bouffant skirt, and my adoration and emotions were beyond anything I had ever felt before. As I looked at Jessie she anticipated my thoughts, and we both

Dale and children Cary and Barbara performing, 1958

knew that if we could convince our shy little girl to join the act, she could be a show-stopper. I asked her to rehearse a George M. Cohan medley with us, but did not insist she perform unless she wanted to. Meanwhile, just in case, we prepared a costume for her to complement our own: a white derby hat with sequins, a short cane, and white gloves.

At Nippersink's club, Cary and I opened our act by singing a duet of the difficult and popular "Rumania, Rumania." Barbara listened and watched intently, mouthing the lyrics of our routines as she sat ringside with Jessie. I could tell that she was struggling with her decision. As we got closer to our George M. Cohan medley, I saw Jessie handing Barb her props and encouraging her to join us on stage. As she walked towards us, the audience "oo'd and aa'd." Our little 4-year-old trouper shocked everyone with her courage. She had always been so shy, hiding behind Jessie when visitors dropped in at our home, and yet here she was, standing bravely on stage with typical show-biz gutsiness. I guess she inherited some of my genes after all.

In my mind, I began to mull over the heart of a performer. To the layman, an actor-entertainer who could step before an audience and emote had to be either an extrovert or some kind of egotist. This is not necessarily true, for I had known many artists who were completely the opposite of their professional images. Many were introverts, withdrawn, and sometimes just plain scared! I had heard that the great Caruso—acclaimed as the world's greatest operatic tenor—sometimes sobbed backstage before a performance. It wasn't until he sang his first notes on stage, that he calmed down enough to give his usual outstanding performance. Many was the time in vaudeville, when I watched performers in the wings praying and kissing *mezuzas*, or crossing themselves before facing their audiences. It really took guts, talent, and a lot of heart to be a performer.

I watched with pride as our little Barb sang and acted out her part at Nippersink; my mind was flooded with thoughts of the past and future. Deep emotions welled up in my heart, and it was all I could do to keep from shedding tears of love right on stage. I felt grateful to Almighty God for welding our lives together in our great mutual interest to entertain. Now, we could perform as a team and a family, and enjoy each other as audiences watched in admiration.

It didn't really matter whether Cary or Barb would ever become professionals. Jessie and I had witnessed too much heartbreak and disappointment in many show business "hopefuls," to nurture frustrating illusions about our kids becoming stars. What *did* matter to us was the warmth and common bond that such a relationship could bring to all of us as a family. It had been some years now since three Linds performed together. Now both my brothers were back again in the guise of my children. At least, that's how I felt. I remembered how Joel Grey started as a youngster with his father, Mickey Katz, and ended up on Broadway. The same was true for one of our greatest entertainers, Sammy Davis, Jr., when as just a little tyke he joined his uncle's act, tapping away as he danced like an adult trouper.

As we continued our show at Nippersink, my heart raced wildly. We went through our paces from "Swanee" to "California, Here I Come," singing, dancing, and kidding the audience as they stomped with approval. Then a wild idea hit me. I put Barb on a stool so everyone could see her. She was shivering from either the air conditioning or nervousness. Someone from ringside handed me a mink stole. I put it over her shoulders, and it hung all the way down to her toes. The audience roared! Then she looked at me with her big, brown eyes as I began singing, "Around the World I've Searched For You." I never heard an audience so quiet. The moment was poignant, dramatic, and yet comic, and no one knew whether to laugh or cry.

When the song was over, I asked Cary how the Jews came over to this country from the old world, and he answered, *"Yiddle* by *yiddle"*—a pun meaning both "Jew by Jew" and "little by little"). Then I turned to Barb and said, "Okay, honey, tell me, why can't they keep Jews in jail?" When Barb answered, "Because they eat lox," the audience exploded!

I looked at Jess and both of us knew we were rich beyond description. After it was all over, someone asked Barb what she had liked best about the performance. She immediately replied, "I loved the applaudience!" That was the inspired phrase that came from her little heart, and I vowed to make it the title of my autobiography!

We worked in shows as a trio from then on.

Chapter 35

FULFILLMENT— AND GRIEF

Meanwhile, I turned down an offer from Joe Glazer, owner of Associated Booking Agency and well-known for being Billie Holiday's manager, to work as a single in Vegas for five thousand dollars a week. Joe thought I was crazy! Maybe I was—but I was already enjoying a different kind of life with Jessie and the kids, and certainly a more stable one. My decision to refuse such a lucrative offer weighed heavily on me for weeks. I felt that accepting Glazer's offer would mean returning to the old grind. I was in my forties now and the thought of starting all over again as a single, with a new repertoire and new management, would bring new stresses into my life.

All performers knew that in Vegas, one had to be the "best of the best," and to be *that* I would need new arrangements of the latest hit songs, with costly orchestrations, and a whole new wardrobe. Also, I would be competing with big names like Wayne Newton, Robert Goulet and others. In Chicago, everyone accepted me as I was, even if I sang with just a piano player or small combo. More importantly, it would mean separation from Jessie, the kids, my parents, and the rest of my family. Glazer would probably be booking me around the country following Vegas, and I didn't relish the idea of living out of a suitcase again. Of course, the money, the glamour and the excitement would all be there for me…but at what price? I would be so absorbed in my new career that it would mean neglecting so many other important aspects of my life.

When I first met with Glazer in his New York office, I brought recordings of my performances on Phil's television show, hoping that he could secure a television contract for me in New York or Hollywood, on the basis of those six months of performances for CBS. That would have meant a more secure home life for me and my family, in one place and one city. Glazer's forté, however, was not in television, but in the night club field. Clubs were a difficult, night-after-night regimen, and in my present stage of life, moving around the country again was not the kind of life I envisioned.

As the years progressed I knew I had made the right decision. The only time I left Chicago was to do one-night concerts out of town, and I always rushed home the next day. I kept busy constantly, with a myriad of engagements and a full social life.

In 1966, I needed a new challenge. I yearned for my own club. I remembered my father's words about venturing into strange fields of endeavor. But my years in nightclubs made me feel confident that I could make a success of it. My name was strong and I was still in prime voice. My own place, with a dinner and entertainment venue, could be the exact formula Chicagoans would flip for.

I let the word out in Chicago that I was interested, and the first call I received was from the managers of the new Chez Paree. They had taken over the old Silver Frolics, re-named it, and completed the extensive refurbishing, only to close in less than sixty days. The heyday of the big spender was over, and it was now obvious that success required the right prices, an ideal location, and a lot of good luck.

Several times, my lawyer and I went through the old and shuttered Chez, on Fairbanks Court in "The Loop," and both of us sensed a kind of foreboding in the atmosphere. Our senses must have been correct, for a few months later, after we refused the deal, the building was torn down. The Chez had been a terrible fire hazard. We would have to wait a bit longer for the right situation.

Fulfillment—and Grief

Dale Lind's Pavillion, 1965

Months later, I received a phone call from the proprietor of a very exclusive and plush restaurant called "Le Pavillon." Located in the northern suburb of Northbrook, it had a marvelous reputation for French cuisine. The proprietor also boasted of a distinguished and affluent clientele. I was intrigued because the Pavillon possessed an atmosphere of elegance and pomp that formed the perfect setting for my dream place.

After weeks of negotiation, Le Pavillon was mine. I was filled with hope and enthusiasm as I took over the reins. Now I began putting my ideas to work...

While diners enjoyed outstanding cuisine in our French dining room, I had the other side of the building remodeled for banquets and shows. It had all the necessary decor for a rambling type of supper club. I was determined to bring back the warmth and informality of the old 5100 Club and Chez Paree days. I began my show policy by inaugurating Wednesday nights as "Celebrity Night." Everyone thought I was out of my mind because nightclub business during the week had declined drastically in the Chicago area.

As the weeks and months went on, my 400-seat club overflowed with crowds, so I added weekend shows as well. The format of two main attractions had succeeded, and business was booming. In every show I sang songs of the day as well as ethnic ones for Italian, Irish, and Jewish audiences. We almost always presented a comedy star of the week. We also catered to parties with special celebrations with free champagne flowing nightly. The Pavillon became one of the hottest spots in Chicagoland as celebrities from all walks of life began frequenting my restaurant.

As with all good, however, there is always tragedy—and when my mom was rushed to Michael Reese Hospital, seriously ill with anemia, we geared ourselves for the worst. Murray, too, had been seriously ill with a strange malady called "Polymyositis"—a mysterious deteriorating muscle disease—and was in the midst of trying to overcome his sudden misfortune. Seeing them both in such a terrible state just about broke me down completely.

One fateful morning I felt somebody hovering over me as I lay sleeping. The presence near me was so strong that it awakened me from my deep slumber. As I looked up, my sister Selma's face was staring down at me. I could sense she was in an awful state. She then quickly informed me about Mom's critical condition. She was sinking in a coma and kept asking for me constantly. I was the only one in the family missing, and she knew it. I did not know where Jessie was – I always slept late because I had terrible hours at the Pavillon. Jessie, an early riser, would always go somewhere with her friends, or shop. I left her a note telling her about Mom, dressed quickly, and was in my car in a matter of minutes.

When I finally reached Mom's bedside she was barely holding on. I grasped her cold hands and yelled into her ear, "Mama, it's me, Dale. Can you hear me? I'm here! I love you, Mom!" Tears ran down my cheeks as she heaved her last gasping breath. Her face became very white and shone like a halo, as if she was embraced by an angel.

After months of suffering, she was finally at peace. As much as my ideology filled me with comforting thoughts as to her heavenly abode, my emotions gave way as I joined the rest of the family in grieving our loss. By now, Dad was impossible to control. He was a total wreck, and no matter how much all of us tried to console him, he kept repeating, "*Oy, kinderlach,* what am I going to do now without her?"

It is tragic when children cannot fully comprehend the blessing of a mother and father while they are alive. But it is even a greater tragedy when we realize their irreplaceable value. My only consolation in losing Mama, was that perhaps the Divine One could use the services of a true angel! Her reward as a great *Yiddishe Mame* was now in God's Hands. To describe her, I thought of the scriptures that speaks of a "A Woman of Valor" that we call an Ayshes Chayil.

She was that and more to all the family and her memory will be in our hearts and minds forever.

"A Woman of Valor"

*A good wife who can find?
The heart of her husband trusts in her
and nothing shall he lack.
She renders him good and not evil
all the days of her life.
She opens her hand to the needy
and extends her hand to the poor.
She is robed in strength and dignity
and cheerfully faces whatever may come.
She opens her mouth with wisdom,
her tongue is guided by kindness.
She tends to the affairs of her household
and eats not the bread of idleness.
Her children come forward and bless her,
her husband, too, praises her:
Many women have done superbly,
but you, Mom, surpassed them all.*

I left the hospital depressed, and drove down Edens Expressway towards home, thinking deeply of my loss. My mother was gone forever. My eyes welled up with tears and I could hardly see. Suddenly, I heard a loud noise and found myself off the side of the road, stunned. As I sat there waiting to awake from my stupor, there was a tap on the window. I looked up to find my brother-in-law, Bob Platt, looking in at me and saying, "Dale, Dale!" Fortunately, he had just happened to be driving by, and had seen my car on the side of the road. I opened the window and he asked,

"Are you all right?"

"I guess I'm okay," I answered groggily.

"You don't have a concussion?"

"Why would I have a concussion?"

"Look." He pointed at the fractured windshield. It was cracked from side to side, obviously from my forehead, but I didn't have a scratch on me. I was perfectly fine, inside and out. Bob continued, "You must have hit a rock or something because you went onto the shoulder." Then we both realized I was not wearing my seat belt. Obviously, when I left the hospital I was in a daze.

Later, when I thought about the whole incident, I wondered, "With thousands of cars on the expressway, how could Bob be there for me at precisely *that* moment?" Here was another miracle in my life. Once again, I had proof that Someone was watching over me...maybe this time it was Mom...

Chapter 36

AN ACT OF GOD—
THE STING OF FATE

In 1966, I began getting long distance calls from stars who were anxious to appear at my club. When my old friend Henny Youngman called to tell me he was coming through Chicago, I welcomed him with great fanfare. We had worked together in Vaudeville and had a great respect and admiration for each other. Needless to say, we were a smash together.

Newcomers and future stars also looked to my place, as a fill-in spot, and they appreciated the special treatment I accorded them. Remembering my struggling days, I issued orders to all my staff to treat all performers royally!

Even though the shows were a great success, I had terrible problems behind the scenes. When I took over the club, I hadn't realized it was such an old building and that repair and maintenance expenses would mount. It seemed like the greater volume we produced, the more expenses we incurred with repairs. I never knew a building could be over-volumed, but ours was catastrophic. Electrical and kitchen equipment kept breaking down, air-conditioning had to be replaced, and the roads leading into the club were sorely in need of repair. Gross income figures meant nothing compared to the weekly outlay of expenses. I had meeting after meeting with my accountants, and still there seemed to be an undercurrent working against me that I couldn't control. I thought to myself, "Again, more stumbling blocks to overcome? Will there ever be smooth sailing in anything I undertake?"

Applaudience: The Autobiography of Dale Lind

Comedy star Henny Youngman appears with Dale at the Pavillon, 1966

In the meantime, business kept increasing. Now, the "Underworld" became aware of the great business we were doing, and began pressing me for involvement. I ignored them. I called an architect friend of mine and asked him to draw up plans for additional facilities. I had dreamed of a dinner theatre restaurant *a la* Drury Lane, on the South Side of Chicago. They had an operation similar to mine, with a larger catering capacity and a huge theatre, which was my dream.

I placed a call to Tony DeSantos, the owner, and invited him to the Pavillon. When he caught my show he was flabbergasted! Then I told him of my plans to build a theater-in-the-round and asked him if he would be interested in a theatre partnership. Certainly he had the know-how and the connections I needed for a successful operation. As we talked, I sensed that maybe he was not the sole boss, that he would have to get the okay from his backers or investors in Drury Lane. When Tony called me, it was thumbs down. They were doing a fantastic business on their own and were not interested in a Northside operation.

My architect and I had an exciting new concept for a circular showroom and lounge. I also wanted our new facilities to be a "wedding-city," with shops for flowers, invitations, a bakery, orchestra representatives, and a choice of a kosher caterer.

As plans were completed, we began negotiating for a two-million dollar loan. My accounting firm assured me we'd have no trouble getting approved. Our volume figures would be proof positive of the need for expansion. I was banking all my hopes and dreams on that loan, and I was convinced that the larger volume in a new building would overcome the losses I was now sustaining.

Suddenly, the mortgage and loan departments of banks and other financial institutions began to tighten up. The economy was in a slump. Newspapers were filled with discouraging market reports. We were turned down continually. As the months passed and the losses kept growing, my hopes for new financing declined. Talks of another depression were in the air and filled me with horrible memories of Black Tuesday in '29.

When I was approached again and again by the underworld, I was so depressed that I agreed to hear their proposition. In the quiet of my office I listened to them assuring me they could get the money needed in twenty-four hours. They knew of my expansion plans and told me the Pavillon would become the outstanding operation of its kind.

I began to weaken. I was desperate and couldn't bear the thought of losing my club. When I asked them who would be floating the loan, they said it was none of my business. When they told me what they expected in return for the loan, I called a meeting with my lawyer and associates. I also called my brother Phil who had some powerful connections. One of his dearest friends, a jeweler, had fenced some jewelry for "the boys." Phil said he would check it out and get back to me. Meanwhile, I had given him the telephone number of the men who approached me and were now waiting for my answer.

I thought back to the many times different members of the underworld had visited my restaurant. They were always well dressed with bejeweled wives and families. Invariably they suggested to me—and very nicely—that I needed better uniformed car-hikers for the valet service for our clients, nicer cigarette machines, younger and prettier check-room girls, and better uniforms for our workers. I was able to pull some strings, time and time again, to get them off my back by calling some of my influential Jewish friends whom I always entertained royally in my club. But these were the real "big boys," the Las Vegas hotel builders. I was frightened, and in a quandary.

When Phil called back and said to me, "I have it on good authority that the best thing for you to do is to put a lock on the door." Those words penetrated my heart like a knife. Phil continued, "If you go through with this, your life will never be your own. Their families will come in and take over. You will also have to be at their every beck and call, singing your heart out. I know its hard, Dale, to give it all up, but the alternative—to go on—is worse. Think hard about it, and let me know."

After hours of deliberation, I went home to meditate. I sat in my study, searching my mind. "Would all the material success in the world be worth the price I'd have to pay?" What they really wanted me for was my name and a legitimate front. I finally went to bed but awoke in the middle of the night in a cold sweat. Everything in me was saying, "Don't do it, don't do it!" I wrestled with my decision till dawn. I was afraid for my family, too, and most of all I feared becoming a pawn for "the boys." That kind of pressure would kill me.

When I finally decided against them, they were shocked, as they knew my tottering circumstances. Their farewell remark was, "You've got guts, we'll say that for you." Then they left, mumbling about my probable downfall.

I was determined to make one more last effort to raise the money I needed. I had already put every dollar I owned into it. A couple of business friends came to my aid, but the timing was off. It was too late, and impossible to stem the tide. As a final blow, in 1967, the biggest snowstorm in Chicago's history struck with all its ferocity. The roof caved in, and my dreams were buried in ice and snow. The roads were out of commission, the water froze, and all electricity was knocked out. Parties were automatically canceled, and we were stuck with the food, liquor and all the other preparations—an unbelievable loss. We were forced out of business by an act of God. Still, we thought our closing would be temporary.

When I took over The Pavillon, I had negotiated a 20-year lease with the landlord. Now that I was in trouble, I called him and asked if he would repair the building so we could continue to operate. Although he was receiving a large amount of rent from me, he was adamant about not investing in repairs, and said, "I'd rather sell the property." Now I was convinced that the Pavillon was *kaput*. Months later, he sold it to the Sheraton Hotel chain, and they gutted the entire building to put up their own.

I grieved about my loss in the privacy of my home. I walked the floors at night, racked with worry and disappointment. I met with two friends who had sunk their hard-earned money into my hopeless condition. Somehow, I would pay them back. It was a catastrophic end to my dream of dreams.

I tried to console myself. I thought of what Jessie was telling intimate friends. Sarcastically, she assured them that if her hair wasn't dyed red, she'd be stark white from all my ventures. Some joke!! What were those five words again? *"And this, too, shall pass."*

Chapter 37

THE SHOW MUST GO ON

When "Kup's Column" in the Chicago Sun-Times printed the news of our closing down, all hell broke loose! Our home was bedlam as brides and grooms, heads of organizations, and others who had scheduled parties months in advance at the Pavillon, panicked. I felt as if the whole world had turned upside down.

Jessie, my secretary, Helen Miller, and I talked ourselves hoarse on the telephone trying to find other available banquet space for our clients. There were a thousand details that had to be rearranged, including our dinner shows. We booked weddings and bar-mitzvahs into restaurants, clubs, hotels, and other establishments. The constant ringing of the phone almost drove us mad—it was all we could do to keep our sanity. Some of those who could have helped us in many ways ran like rats from a sinking ship. They were the leeches, who had stuck around only as long as things were going well.

One of my closest friends offered me his checkbook and asked me to fill in the amount I needed. It was gratifying to know there was someone who cared that much. I declined his help with thanks.

My biggest worry was my voice. I was concerned that all the aggravation and emotional pressure would affect me vocally. I used to think that I had a voice, but through the years I discovered that the voice had me. And now, more than ever, I had to look to my voice and my show business experience for my future security. Whenever I had a few minutes to spare, I'd vocalize to see if it was still functioning. So far, it was. That gave me some comfort, because my voice was the only commodity I had left that could sustain me through this awful time.

Applaudience: The Autobiography of Dale Lind

Dale entertaining at Chicago's College Inn at the Sherman House, 1968

Through the grapevine I was told that the old College Inn and the Sherman House had been taken over by Gerald Kaufman of New York City. I also knew that his weekend shows were dying. I called and made an appointment with Kaufman.

When I showed him my files of advance bookings at the Pavillon, he was shocked. They numbered in the hundreds. He signed me immediately for six months. There was absolutely no gamble on his part, or mine, for we had bona fide contracts with responsible groups who were loyal followers. Now I could fulfill my contractual obligations in a world-famous showplace. Still, it was increasingly difficult for me to do the shows as I kept remembering my beautiful Pavillon. I missed having my own club. It was hard to let go of a dream I had lived with for so many years, to finally achieve it, and then to lose it. It was all too short-lived. Was it all predestined?

It was torture to walk on stage to an audience that was supposed to have been at the Pavillon. When I joked about it, that I was saying *Kaddish* (the mourner's prayer) for it, they laughed out loud, while I was crying on the inside. Those were "Laugh, Clown, Laugh" performances, as I sang my guts out and thought my heart would burst. Still, when they applauded and cheered me, I found new courage and took refuge in their love. Then I remembered a saying, "For every door that closes, another one opens." It would be interesting to know what the future held for me. Already I had been through so much. What next?

Someone once asked a comedian friend of mine, "Tell me—why must the show go on?" He answered, "Because there's money in the box office, you idiot."

Chapter 38

OVERCOMING ADVERSITY

It was now January of '67. Six months had passed since the closing of my club. I kept thinking about the number of hours I spent at The Pavillon. In less than two years, my hours accumulated into what would be like ten normal work years. Some of those hours were marvelous and rewarding. I certainly didn't mind the heavy show schedule. That was the fun part. But the animosity I suffered when people wanted a better table and I couldn't oblige, the petty personal grievances, the numerous times employees didn't show up, or when the septic tanks backed up. All of it was a constant headache. I recall the times that cars were backed up in long lines waiting to get to the front door, or when a customer came in screaming about a dented fender or getting stuck in the snow, and the numerous disturbances that were always so troubling. There was always some kind of complaint from a dissatisfied patron. But then there were those who raved and raved about the specialties of our wonderful chefs, like the canaloni, our steaks, and our outstanding fish delicacies. There was always entertainment in the lounge. The bar was jam-packed and our shows were S.R.O. with raves from the newspapers and Holiday Magazine. Who could have had a better combination of winners?

"Celebrity Nights," our show nights, had become so popular that celebrations for weddings and numerous other occasions were held then. We greeted these special parties with complimentary champagne and special acknowledgements.

The laughter and noise during dinner spoke for our success. And later, the applause for the performers was deafening. In every way, our formula was clicking—except for the thievery. We discovered—too late—that waiters were walking out with cash that should have gone into the register. What crooks! My bartenders, who I thought were so honest, were having a field day ringing up lesser amounts and pocketing the difference.

After the club closed, one of my loyal employees came to visit me at my home and revealed so many things I should have known before. He told me that he never expected the Pavillon would close its doors. Because of the tremendous amount of business we were doing, he thought we could overcome the thievery. Now that the Pavillon was no more, now that nobody could call him a snitch, he felt duty-bound to tell me everything. It was he who told me that while I was doing shows, employees were raiding the kitchen. Nothing was sacred and nothing was spared; steaks and other goodies were looted and put into their cars and trunks. I asked him, "Where were my managers? Where were my chefs? Were they all involved?"

"Well," he answered, "they just looked away, not wanting to expose the guilty parties." I was stunned. I should have suspected something was wrong when I discussed my tremendous food bills with my accountants. But it seemed right with the huge turnouts. Even my buyers were cheating, as they favored certain food and liquor companies because of their kick-backs. Ah—we get smart too late!

In the aftermath, my greatest satisfaction was that I was able to go on performing, while the crooks were out of work. The thousands of dollars that were stolen and went down the drain might have kept us in the black. Again, too late!

The only compensation for me was that nothing, and no one, could destroy the power of my name and reputation. That would keep me going as long as I lived. I would survive, no matter what. I had the good fortune to perform at the Pavillon for thousands of people, and had won their acclamation. That, alone, would surely bode well for my future.

After some weeks, I thought I had weathered the emotional shock of losing my club, until one night I awoke with excruciating pain. Jessie was scared to death and called my doctor to come running. As I moaned and groaned, I began to bargain with God. "Please God, don't let this be a heart attack. I'll settle for an ulcer, anything but a heart attack. In fact, I'll accept any reasonable facsimile, but please, God, no heart trouble. I have to go on singing." Jessie must have thought I was crazy! But to me, an ulcer was the lesser of two evils. Besides, since the beginning of time, Jews have always debated with God. I had every right to barter, especially considering the fact that I didn't ask to come here in the first place. But now that I was here, why not try to get the best deal? I used to sing a song called, "A Debate With God," which ended with the *Kaddish*, the mourner's prayer, and that's what frightened me.

As I suffered, my mind began to wander. I remembered how my dear father would take his three boys to Orchard Street, on the East Side of New York, a week before the High Holidays. This was the street that ran for blocks and blocks, filled with push-cart peddlers, like Chicago's Maxwell Street. Peddlers did business according to their own codes, and they expected you to barter, as that was the way in the old country. It was all part of the fun. You were practically forced and dragged into the stores by shills, and before you could say "No!" you were already being fitted—with accessories to match.

Orchard Street operators had built-in radar, and knew just what you were looking for. I remember once when each of us tried on a blue gabardine suit. I noticed the tag said $18. Pop paid no attention to tags, and he said to the merchant, "I'll give you $18 for all three suits."

The merchant shot back, "Vot, you crazy? It cost *me* more. But I'll tell you vot I'll do. Dese soots ver ordered fa a speshel poyson. But I'll let you take dem fa $12 itch."

My father grabbed us. "*Koom, kinder,* come kids, we're leaving. This man is crazy."

"Jost a second," the merchant yelled. "Don' get so oxited. Orright, I'll looz moni, bot tek di soots fa $8 itch."

My father, now angrier, looked right into the eyes of the merchant and said, "Look, Mr., uh–"

"Pincus!" the man yelled.

"All right, Mr. Pincus, my last offer is $18 for all three. Take it or leave it. Come boys."

At this point, Pincus grabbed my father by the arm and yelled, "Boy, do you drive a hod bahgen. Tek dem arredi. I kent stend to see soch byoodiful boyes vit soch olt cloze." Now *that's* what I call bartering!

By now, I was rolling on the bed with terrible pain. I was in agony as the doctor examined me. I was feverish and nervous, fearing the worst. My only comfort was my everlasting faith and deep trust in our family doctor, Sheldon Cogan. He was a thorough internist and expert diagnostician. I knew that as soon as he knew what was wrong, he would immediately give me something to alleviate my suffering. For a moment my mind wandered. I thought, "How horrible for a woman giving birth with such pain." Suddenly I appreciated Jessie more, and as I turned to her, her face was filled with worry.

Meanwhile, Shelley had prescribed medication over the phone to our pharmacist. They grasped the nature of the emergency and delivered it in a matter of minutes. As soon as I downed the pills, I felt drowsy. I hadn't slept all night, and whatever he gave me did the trick; I fell into a sound sleep.

When I woke up four hours later, the pain had subsided, and Jessie drove me to his office. I felt like someone had kicked me in the stomach. Shelley examined me thoroughly, putting me through a cardiogram, X-rays, and other tests. I was too weak to pester him with questions. I figured if it was good news, it would be welcome, and if it was bad news, it could certainly wait.

When Shelley called the next day, he told me I had what is commonly known as a hiatal hernia. I was extremely thankful that my heart was okay, but I marveled at the fact that a small pin-hole in my diaphragm could cause such misery. It was inconceivable! He then gave me a list of what not to eat, which I neglected to follow as I felt better. After two more attacks, I decided to behave myself.

Now it was time to pick up the pieces of my hectic and crazy life — if not for me, then at least for the sake of my family. I had sorely neglected them during the Pavillon years. I was seldom at home, and when I was, I was preoccupied with business. We used to have such great times together. Since The Pavillon, there hadn't been time to enjoy so many little things, the scrabble games, the theatre, and working out new show routines with the kids. On Sunday mornings we often stood in our hallway as if on stage, but in our pajamas and robes.

I missed the times when Cary played the piano and we'd all sing together, improvising wild, amazing harmony, until midnight. We used to say, "What other family is nuts enough to sing that late? Only the Linds." I thought about how it would feel to be able to go on a trip with my family without worrying about the business back home.

I had neglected my parents, too. It had been a long time since my father's contented *"Oy, siz a mechaye* (such a pleasure)," had echoed through the *Shvitz* hot-room at the North Avenue Baths. It was wonderful spending time with him, laughing and joking with the other *shvitzers*. When Dad laughed out loud, his whole body shook, as his booming voice echoed off the tile walls. My adoration of him had no bounds, because he made me realize how wonderful life can be when father and son share such memorable experiences.

As for my mother, she was our best audience! Whatever comedy *shtick* we did always convulsed her. She would laugh so hard that tears ran from her eyes. And we laughed with her, at our own jokes yet.

With my problems now behind me, I could concentrate fully on what I wanted to do with the rest of my life. I wondered if I should continue cantoring or look to new horizons. Until I could decide, my future was on hold...

Chapter 39

Eulogy For My Father

In June of 1973, my father's time with us was coming to an end. He was in great pain when he entered Michael Reese Hospital for tests. He never left the hospital. When I visited him during his last days, he was worn out, stark white, wan and frail. I knew it wouldn't be long. As he lay in his bed, I tried to comfort him, saying that he would be with Mom. He replied, "I hope so."

His whole life flashed before me at that moment. I remembered my parents' struggles as immigrants. I recalled how Dad worked in a garment factory until he won his first cantorial job on Allen Street, on the East Side of New York City. I remember how he answered Barb when she asked him what he had done when he first got to America. "What do you think," he answered, "I organized a choir!"

I remembered how he grew in stature, and eventually became President of New York's 400-member Cantors Association, and how hard he worked to make it more successful.

I recalled how hard he labored with children for his choir, and taught them how to read music. I remembered so many adversities that he overcame through his faith and persistence.

I remembered all the great singers, cantors, choir directors and opera stars who owed him so much for the compositions he wrote for their special needs. All he had to know was their vocal range, and the melodies poured out of him.

The frivolity we had together, the humor he displayed, the time he took to play with us, and the laughter we enjoyed together are engraved in my memory. Whenever I was near him, I could feel his special warmth,

Father of Lind brothers, Cantor Joshua Lind 1955

love and gentleness. There was a radiance around him that shone forth like the light of God's stars in Heaven.

Of course, he had his moods, like all humans. He was stubborn when he felt he was right, but most of the time he was jolly, and a delight to be with.

At the crack of dawn he was always composing, even while still in his pajamas. And when he dressed, he was immaculate right down to the color of his socks.

Those who knew my father would agree that he was an amazing man. Not only was he a great tenor, but he had the innate ability of expressing through his music the woes and joys of our people. His compositions for cantor and choir were stunning and profound, and nurtured the needs of cantors and choral directors for all of his lifetime.

Now that he is gone, Dad's memory and works are being brought to the fore by one of his former constituents. Dad had given many of his works to Neil Levin, a musicologist and masterful choral conductor who knew Dad in Chicago. Levin is now the Artistic Director for the Milken Archive Foundation, which is recording Jewish masterpieces from around the world. Levin knew the value of Dad's compositions and has included many of them in the Archive, recording them with world-class choirs in New York and London. Somehow, I feel that Dad is looking down and *kvelling* proudly.

Thinking of my father, of blessed memory, always gave me the impetus I needed to lift myself up and out of the doldrums. He was always my inspiration! For that, I will always be grateful, and count myself lucky.

He *did* live to enjoy many special honors accorded him from time to time. In the early 60's, the Midwestern Cantors and Ministers Association honored Dad at a banquet at the (now defunct) Morrison Hotel. Present at this Honor Evening were many dignitaries from all walks of life. There were politicians such as Jack Arvey, judges such as Abraham Marovitz, many distinguished cantors and rabbis, including representatives from powerful and influential organizations such as *B'Nai Brith,* and the many friends Dad had made through the years. Recently, through a cousin of mine in Pittsburgh, Myrna Backal, I was informed that a tape recording of that evening of tribute had been circulating around the country. When I received a cassette copy from Myrna, labeled, *A Tribute to Joshua Lind,* I was stunned. As a young man, my own record producer, Barry Serota, had taped the entire proceedings and was listed on the album. I called him immediately to get more copies.

When I listened to the highlights, I was overwhelmed. I had forgotten that the Three Lind Brothers had started the evening with two fabulous renditions: one an Israeli medley, and the other our special version of *"Eili-Eili."* My dad closed the evening with a special chant he had written, and I cried as I listened to his glorious interpretation of the liturgy. His voice penetrated my spirit, and I was so touched by the oration of praise from those who spoke that night. That was when I realized, more than ever, that I had been born to a master cantorial creator . . . in fact, as others had proclaimed him, "a true genius."

At his funeral, the chapel overflowed with artists, doctors, cantors, rabbis, choir directors and singers. It was a tribute of which to be proud. Although only five foot four, he was really a giant of a man, to which all who remember him can attest to. Did we love, respect, admire and honor him?—more than I could ever describe. He was a true son of God!

Chapter 40

LIFTING MYSELF UP

I felt the need for rejuvenation and a new stimulus! My batteries were running down, and my motor needed a tuneup, so I began reading my faith books again: all the picker-uppers like "Success Through A Positive Mental Attitude" by W. Clement Stone. I felt close to him as I read his words of wisdom. Clem, as he liked to be called by his friends, had frequented my Pavillon, and we had become friends. As I read his books again and again, my admiration and respect for him grew with every page.

Once again, I began developing a positive mental outlook, as he preached. As the days went on, I began to feel restored and revitalized. Slowly but surely, I was burying my bitterness and regaining my enthusiasm and confidence. I remembered the wisdom of our sages who preached that a bad chapter had to be concluded before a new one could begin. A turbulent phase of my life was ending, and now, I hoped, I could look forward to a far better future, and certainly a more peaceful one. After all, I was only in my 50s, and I was restless enough to look to new horizons with new challenges! I had been living in a world of so much glamour and celebrity that I could never go back to the mundane. It would bore me to death.

At times like these, I missed my buddies in show business, and the excitement of it all. Even with its uncertainties, we had a camaraderie that was priceless and irreplaceable. I felt a deep need for a more meaningful existence. But how could I follow all that I'd done? In show biz, when there was a great act performing before us we would always say, "That's a tough act to follow." Now, I had to follow myself. It was time for me to find an inner strength and a new inspiration. I prayed, I meditated, and I asked God for guidance. And somehow, I knew I was entering a more spiritual phase of my life.

Some nights I would sit in the kitchen, inhaling steam for a congested throat and watching the late-late-late Western movie on television. Barb would come in from a date and we'd play Tableen, a kind of Russian Casino card game we learned from my father. I think we played cards through the end of every old movie ever shown on television! I still couldn't see much of Cary, for he was away most of the time at Brandeis University.

I turned to my family. Keeping the family together, and in close touch, was always a priority with Jessie and me. Watching our grandchildren, nieces, and nephews growing up was one of the fun things in life. To participate with them at school functions, shows, and other interests made us feel like a permanent part of their lives. To have them participate with us, no matter what the occasion, was even more fulfilling.

As the elders of the family, Jessie and I ran the Passover *Seder* dinners, the ceremonial meal accompanying the holiday observance, year after year. It was no easy chore for Jessie to prepare dinner for thirty to forty people, but she did it all with love and dedication. What a privilege for all of us to sit at one table and break *matzah* together.

Always well organized, and a terrific cook and baker, Jessie prepared everything months in advance. From the matzo-ball soup and the traditional brisket with all the trimmings, to her fabulous desserts, our freezers were loaded with Jessie's goodies. Her mistakes were also legendary! How she would turn a mistake into a wondrous miracle— even better than the original—will always remain a mystery to all the family. The kids urged her to write a recipe book called "Jessie's Mistakes." Maybe a best seller?

What made our *Seders* unique was the singing. Family members, especially the ones who sang in our synagogue choir, launched into the special Passover songs with great zest, sounding like the "Anvil Chorus" of the *opera Il Trovatore*. There were the traditional melodies of old, along with new versions of a new generation of composers. But our best "fun song" has always been our version of "Go Down Moses," with a rousing "Let My People Go" ending!

The *Yom Kippur* Holiday, a most sacred time in Judaism, is another time when togetherness with family is heartwarming, especially during worship. I always thought it was sad that members of many Jewish families never felt the need to worship together in a synagogue. The lack of that kind of spiritual togetherness is an unfortunate statistic of Jewish life. Still, when it comes to the traditional gastronomical delights, most Jews do get together and celebrate the holidays with family and friends. At the culmination of *Yom Kippur,* we always extended special invitations to non-worshipers as well, to join us at the "Breaking of the Fast" in our home.

Always, there exists the pervading spirit of our parents at times of special need. To this day, I meditate whenever I need direction from Dad, and he is always there for me, in a sort of continuation of our lives together. Such has been the case many times on the pulpit when I was chanting, or when I was composing music for my choir in the quiet of my study. On the pulpit, whenever I felt my energy ebbing, I would think of Dad and voila, I would feel a surge of new found strength. One night, I was writing and composing a new "*Hallelujah*" for my synagogue choir in my study. It was in the wee hours of the morning, and as usual, our house was quiet—no phone calls and no disturbances. That's when I wrote best. As my mind started racing through a powerful march tempo, my whole body pulsated with the rhythm. I was writing faster and faster as the notes burst through in my head.

Suddenly, I began shaking uncontrollably. I put my pen down immediately and just sat there, frightened! I never liked stopping when ideas were coming fast and furious. I had to put it down on paper, then and there, for who knew if that same inspiration would hit me tomorrow? But I had never experienced that kind of emotional reaction before. For some reason, the "*Hallelujah*" tempo was so exciting that I could hear a hundred-voice choir singing in my ear. Thus, my reaction! What now?—I had to top shaking before continuing.

Amazingly, I felt a calming presence standing over me. I heard my father's voice whisper in my ear, "Relax, Dale, I'll get you through this." The whole atmosphere around me was stilled! I felt Dad's calmness in my body as I picked up the pen again and put it to paper, and the awareness of time had left me. When I was finished, and looked at the music I had just written, I knew that Dad and I had written a heavenly masterpiece together. I looked up as his presence left me and said, "Thanks Pop—I love you."

Later, when our choir sang the *"Hallelujah"* with its rousing finish that went into the high C's, our congregation was mesmerized and moved to and fro with the music. Everyone, including the singers, was exhilarated, as was I. My father's spirit would always be present in his music, and I knew that someday it would be recorded and sung throughout the world.

Chapter 41

AND THE YOUNG SHALL LEAD US

The new challenge I needed in my life came in the guise of summer theatre. When a group of youngsters, including Cary and Barbara, asked me if I would consider playing the part of Tevye in Fiddler on the Roof, I jumped at the opportunity. Ranging in age from eighteen to twenty-five, these young people had just organized a summer theatre group made up of their former schoolmates. With no real funding to start with, theirs was a Herculean undertaking with which I was anxious to help. I began by contacting influential friends, and when they responded with checks as Sponsors, "The Ridotto Players" were on their way.

It was the late 1960's, and daily headlines in the newspapers blazed away about how terrible our youth were—that they were dirty, obscene, dope fiends. I was determined to show the world that there was a still greater percentage of good kids, who involved themselves in meaningful and creative endeavors. As I became more of a father figure to them, I was able to gain unusual insight into their dreams and goals. As these talented kids strolled in for auditions, dressed in jeans, I was awed by their energy and gutsiness.

Meanwhile, we had been turned down for Fiddler by the New York Rental Office, which had decided to wait another year before releasing Fiddler rights to community groups. The traveling companies were still packing them in, so why the rush? After deliberating and discussing many shows, we decided on the difficult but beautiful Kismet as our replacement. This was the show that had produced "Stranger In Paradise" and so many other wonderful hit songs.

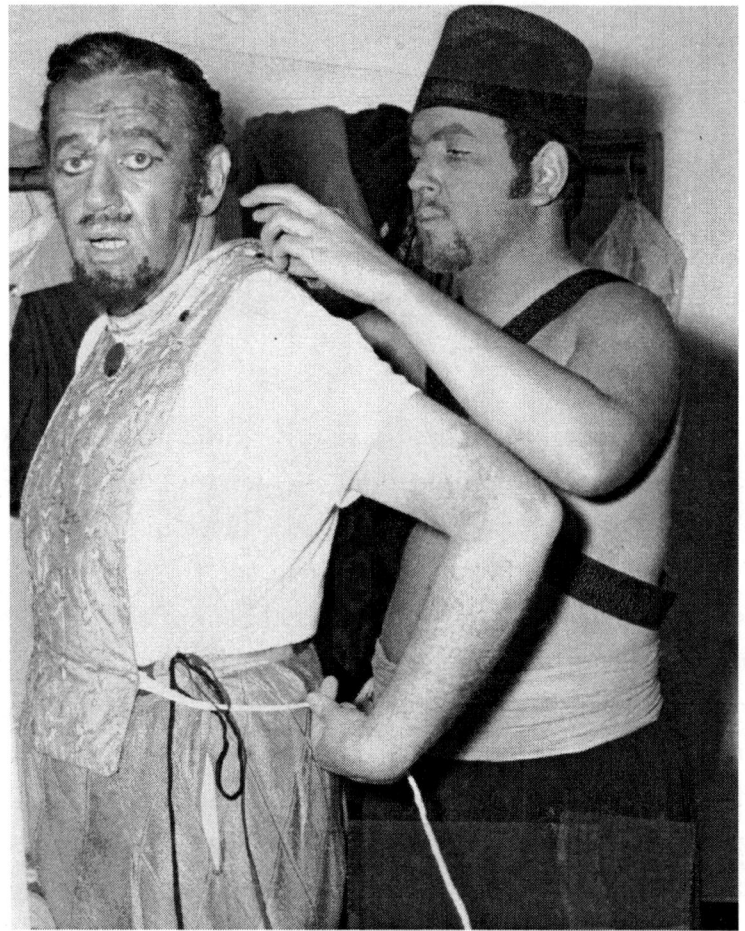

Drssing for "Kismet" opening night, July 13, 1968

To avoid the heavy costs of lumber, costumes and equipment, I again contacted business friends to contribute what they could. I was happy to find that there were still people who cared enough about what we were trying to do, that donated generously to our cause.

Our backstage crews spent days building sets, designing lights and costumes, and working on a hundred other details, while their compatriots in other places were rioting, creating havoc, destruction, and even death. It was a horrendous comparison, as young people bent on destroying our institutions chose to spend their energies in rebellion on the one hand, while our group in a small corner of the suburb of Skokie chose to involve themselves in promoting the arts and bringing culture to Chicagoans.

Now, we needed a public relations man. I thought of my old friend, Paul Montague, who had represented The Lind Brothers at times in Chicago and who handled the press when Liz Taylor and Richard Burton visited our city.

After great effort on our behalf, he informed me that he was meeting with negative response from the media. I was deeply disappointed! It was tragically apparent to me that these kids were too clean and too straight to be newsworthy. My blood boiled, and I was more determined than ever to break through to some good press.

Fortunately, "The Phil Lind Show," a celebrity interview format on local radio, was hot. I appealed to my brother for help, and he slated our principle performers for a half-hour interview. That broke the ice! People stopped me in the streets to congratulate me, and requests for tickets began to soar.

Securing volunteer musicians was a tall order, but the determination of the kids was so great as they spread the word, that thirty-five young musicians came to our rescue. Rehearsing night and day, while their friends were at the

beaches enjoying the summer, was a supreme sacrifice. But in the end, the results were astounding as they were molded into a junior symphony under the direction of Thelma Wilcox, the kids' former high school music teacher.

When rehearsals began, I had to get over my shyness in order to do a love scene. My co-star and I were supposed to embrace and kiss, and then quickly be interrupted by the entrance of the character playing my daughter, Marcinah (Kathy Betts). The first time we rehearsed the scene, and I started kissing my co-star, Marcinah failed to enter on cue. The kiss seemed endless, so, still kissing, and turning red with embarrassment, I started waving one arm, beckoning for Marcinah to enter. On purpose, she entered late, doubled up with laughter, as was everyone else! I was teased for weeks.

As Hajj, the poet, I had a ball "gesticulating" (the title of one of my songs) and singing "Under the Olive Tree." One night, singing "Gesticulate," I was having such a good time, and I felt so extremely good vocally, that at the end of the song, instead of finishing on my usual high F, I went into the tenor register and hit a high A. Thelma looked up from conducting the orchestra and gasped. This was the same woman who, after listening to one of my High Holiday performances, had rolled her eyes and said, "He must do it with mirrors."

Going from Beggar to Emir every night was exhilarating, as I watched my own kids, with one hundred other youngsters, bring pleasure to our audiences. I dreaded our closing night at summer's end. The kids cried and hugged each other and smothered me with their affection and thanks. I had succeeded in closing some of the "Generation Gap." It was very fulfilling to be accepted into the inner sanctums of those wonderful, talented kids!

Chapter 42

RETURNING TO MY SPIRITUAL CALLING

Kismet had inspired me to look for a female partner with whom I could do duets from musicals and different show business venues. For the next few years, I had at least four different singing partners, which created more variety in my shows.

During those years, I was also performing High Holiday Services at the Albany Park Hebrew Congregation. I had to think of new ways to bring back as many of the old members as I could, if only for the High Holidays. Along with some of the officers, I began a barrage of phone calls to everyone who was ever involved with the congregation. When we told them we would have a fabulous choir and outstanding soloists to assist me, they began to make reservations. By the time the holidays arrived, we were sold out. With no parking lot, returning members parked everywhere within a seven-block circle of the synagogue. We convinced everyone that this was a last-ditch effort to save the shul, and they responded accordingly.

I decided to make a great change in the service. The first cantorial prayer on the first day of *Rosh Hashona,* and on *Yom Kippur* Day, was usually sung by the Cantor alone, and was called "*Hineni*" ("Here I Am"). Following ancient cantorial tradition, I walked down the middle aisle toward the pulpit, chanting. But like my father before me, I had always been an innovator. So I thought, "Wouldn't it be a touching moment to have Barbara and Cary join me in parts of the "Hineni"? They were now aged nine and thirteen respectively. It was 1968, and this was an Orthodox congregation. As such, they never allowed women on the pulpit. But Barb was a child. How could they frown on that? I decided that both my children would walk down the middle aisle with me, chanting "*Hineni.*"

The three of us wore new white satin robes and gold-trimmed *yarmulkes*. I began the first part of the prayer alone. When we sang together, there was a hush in the congregation. It was eerie! I began to perspire, and I must admit that for the first time as a cantor, I felt apprehensive. I thought, "Maybe, this time, I made a terrible mistake." As we were approaching the pulpit, a murmuring began from some congregants. One of them whispered, "We don't allow women on the pulpit." Fortunately, the hierarchy were so enchanted with my kids, especially our little nine-year-old singing with such heartfelt cries from deep down in her soul, that they began to "shush" the objectors. "Sh-sh-sh, she's just a little child." I was so relieved. It was revolutionary! It was poignant and dramatic! From then on, we chanted "*Hineni*" as a trio, crying out not just "Here I am," but "Here we are, Dear God!"

After three years of cantoring at Albany Park, the congregation was barely surviving. That's when I decided to run an "All-Star Revue" at McCormick Place, under the auspices of the Congregation.

I used my influence with the newspapers and promoted my revue to the extent where Jewish organizations flooded our office for reservations. It was just the kind of situation they were looking for as a money-maker. Hundreds of groups bought blocks of tickets at a discount, and eventually we were SRO.

The Arie Crown Theatre at McCormick Place had a seating capacity of four thousand seats plus, which was mammoth but beautiful. I hired a large orchestra and featured comedy star Henny Youngman, along with my kids and Salena, my singing partner at that time. Our show was a huge success, and my congregation and outside organizations were delighted with their financial gains.

The following year, I produced another all-star review, at the famed Orchestra Hall. It was always a dream of mine to appear in the same auditorium where all the greatest artists concertized. Henny Youngman co-starred with me again. I recorded the concert on tape and released it as an audio cassette: "Dale Lind at Orchestra Hall." That was a sweet fulfillment for me.

Albany Park was waning as a Jewish neighborhood. Many of the synagogue's members were moving further north to suburban areas, and the elders were retiring to warmer climates. Some bad elements were now living in Albany Park and committing anti-Semitic acts—like breaking the stained glass windows of our congregation and creating havoc while services were in progress. I knew it was time for me to make a change.

I sought out Oscar Brotman and Leonard Sherman who owned the Lincoln Village Theatre in Chicago. They were featuring Yiddish artists in special shows. I met with them to sell them on the idea of running my own High Holiday Services at their theatre. I had read in the Jewish "Sentinel" that there were one hundred thousand unaffiliated Jews in the Chicago area at that time. The three of us agreed that our services would fill a great need in the community. I sought to create an uplifting and traditional atmosphere with a great 24-voice choir, which would spark interest in the unaffiliated in returning to the synagogue.

The theatre had 1500 seats and was in an ideal location. We agreed on terms and proceeded to make our plans. As we began advertising the services on their movie screen, the response was immediate, and reservations began pouring in.

We were nearing a sold-out house, when suddenly a large group of religious leaders representing seventeen congregations, approached Oscar and Leonard and demanded that they cancel our services. Oscar was furious and replied, "Why would you want us to do that?"

Their spokesman answered, "Because you will hurt our congregation attendance, and we'll lose many of our members."

"What a lot of bull," Oscar fired back. "That's the most ridiculous thing I've ever heard. We can only fill 1500 seats while you have thousands. Besides, we are appealing to the unaffiliated who need a service like this in the community. And certainly we don't want or need any of your members."

They left with red faces, embarrassed, but still wouldn't stop harassing both partners. First, they threatened a boycott of the movie theatre. Then they started on a different tack. Knowing that Leonard was deeply involved with the United Jewish Appeal (UJA), they threatened to boycott that organization as well. Because their council represented thousands of Jews and wielded powerful influence, Oscar and Leonard finally succumbed to the threats and canceled their contract with me. They knew it was wrong, and were deeply disappointed that our own religious hierarchy would stoop to blackmail. Oscar and Leonard really had no choice. The pressure was just too great.

When Oscar called me for an emergency meeting, I knew instinctively that something was wrong. When they told me what had happened, I was in a rage. Oscar and Leonard said that since they had broken my contract, I had every right to sue them. However, they told me they felt powerless in their situation. I thought about our friendship, and knew that if I took that kind of action, I would not only hurt the UJA, but the entire Jewish community. No doubt, there would be a rebellion by those who had made reservations, and once it hit the newspapers, rabbis, clergy, and Lord knows who else might get involved. In general, this could become a nasty situation not only because of the injustice of it all, but because it would be a blot on the Jewish hierarchy. I was not about to stir up that kind of controversy, so I told Oscar that given the situation, I understood their decision. I felt strongly that somehow I would find another way, where no one could interfere with my services. But like the song I used to sing about the wandering Jew, "Where Can I Go??"

I was furious, upset and angry because there is no Jewish law prohibiting religious services anywhere, anytime, as long as there is a *minyan*, which in Jewish law means that ten people must be present. When I was a youngster living in New York City, many services took place in Jewish areas. Anyone who wished to run a service on the High Holy Days rented facilities in banquet halls, in the Catskill Mountain hotels and resorts, or held them in their own *shtieblech* (small homes). In a city like New York, with a population of approximately three million Jews, who would dare to stop anybody from worshiping with fellow Jews?

I thought back to World War II, when for a Jewish GI's *yahrzeit*, an annual memorial date for a deceased member of the family, we sought out ten Jews and held a service so the *Kaddish* could be said. On ship, on our way to the Pacific, we met for services in every conceivable location. It is a sin for any Jew not to have a service upon a request by anyone in need. It behooved me as a cantor to bring comfort to those who mourned and to rekindle the spirit of our fathers.

Now there were only six weeks left before the holidays, and I was beside myself. As I sat in my home, I actually cried, thinking, "What am I going to do? There must be a way. God will not forsake me! I must continue to believe! I must have faith!"

I had been in rehearsal with my choir for weeks. I was obligated to them, too, and it was too late for my professional singers to get another job, nor could I, as cantor. How could I possibly not chant on the holiest of days? I had never missed a year, not even when the three of us were in show business. In my despondency, I turned to Jessie to ask her advice. She reminded me of our five words: *"And this, too, shall pass."*

She thought for a while in her calm way, and finally said, "Wait a minute. Honey, I think, maybe, we could rent the Grand Ballroom at the Orrington Hotel in Evanston." As a party consultant, Jessie had run numerous weddings there, and together we had been responsible for bringing in a great deal of business to the hotel.

With no time to waste, I rushed to Evanston, sought out the owner of the hotel, and began negotiations. He was the nicest gentleman I had ever dealt with. He wasn't Jewish, so I explained to him that I was like a "Jewish Billy Graham," with my own following. I told him I was organizing my own independent congregation and would like to rent his ballroom for the High Holidays for many years to come. I also told him that there were congregations who feared my competing with them, and that he would receive letters and disturbing phone calls asking him not

The Ark of the Holy Scrolls (Torahs)

to rent his facilities to me. The clincher came when I told him that the Holidays would bring new exposure to his hotel and its facilities, as well as room reservations on the holidays by many of our orthodox worshippers. He was so pleased, that he immediately signed a contract with me, and assured me of full cooperation in every way.

All the correspondence and phone calls he received from people objecting to my services, went into the waste basket. He resented the personal vendetta against me, and did everything he could to protect me. Needless to say, it eventually stopped and we had triumphed—temporarily. Our son, Cary, now an attorney, secured a state license for me to operate "The Sons of Joshua Independent Congregation," which could function anywhere we wished. We chose to honor my father's name. I prayed that with his blessing from his heavenly place, we would glean only good.

We began an advertising blitz in all the Jewish newspapers. Ticket reservations could only be made at our residence in Skokie. Over the next few weeks, 1100 people stood in line inside and outside our home, to join our synagogue. It was the most gratifying response we could ever have expected in so short a time. Obviously, this was proof positive that we were filling a real need.

Jessie turned the hotel ballroom into a synagogue, with gold and velvet coverings on the pulpit, with abundant flowers everywhere. I had had a special Ark built in the design of a 9-foot tall Star of David, painted with the Ten Commandments and two guardian lions. The star parted in the middle of the Commandments to reveal three magnificent *Torah* scrolls.

Opening the Ark, and carrying or reading from the *Torah*, is considered a great honor. In most synagogues, these honors are given to people who are the most active in the congregation and who contribute the most financially. Our synagogue was different. Because we had no Board of Directors and no contributors, individuals were picked at random to be honored. My good friend, Harold Lipke, was President of *B'Nai Joshua*. Among other duties, he chose the congregants who would receive these honors. At our first service, Jessie was sitting in her seat amongst the other congregants. The man behind her, not knowing who was sitting in front of him, said cynically, "I wonder who you have to know to get an honor?" Jessie heard him and called Harold over to ask him to select the man behind her for the next honor. Harold did, and never had he seen so startled a man! There were no further comments from the rear.

As the years went on, we became a viable and recognized institution in the Jewish Community. We had persevered and succeeded in our purpose to provide affordable and inspirational worship services on the Holy Days. We continued with our services for 27 wonderful years.

Chapter 43

PARTIES & CRUISE SHIPS

Jessie and I, tried to figure out how we could keep in touch with our congregants during the entire year, not just on the High Holidays. We finally came to a decision, and in 1971 we began our own wedding and party consulting firm under the name of "Dale Lind Enterprises." We had already converted a spare bedroom in our home to an office for our congregation, so why not use it for party planning, too? It would not only be a great adjunct for our members, but for others, as well. We were confident that we would succeed in our new venture. It would be exactly what we needed to create a greater friendship not only with our members, but with the entire Jewish community.

As soon as word got out, we began receiving calls from suppliers like florists, orchestras, photographers, calligraphers, and others involved in occasions of every kind. Jessie made contacts with special bakeries for sweet tables, wedding cakes, and specialty items. We were a well-organized team. While I took care of the entertainment, music, and performing at all our functions as cantor, entertainer, and master of ceremonies, Jessie handled the myriad of details, including the wedding rehearsals. I *shlepped* along with her as a helping hand, especially when there were business discussions with hotels.

Jessie certainly had plenty to do teaching Cary, Barbara, and our daughter-in-law, Sandy, how to set up trays with many different fanciful items such as gourmet candies, cookies, and special chocolates. Arranging unique decorations, ice pieces, floral arrangements, and so many more items was also an integral part of our party service.

Applaudience: The Autobiography of Dale Lind

Jessie and Dale relaxing at home, 1975

Guests made their way like "gang-busters" to our magnificently set up sweet tables. Everyone went gaga and shook their heads in amazement. Jessie was one of the first party consultants to add an age-old traditional Yiddish treat to the sweet table: *halvah*, a Turkish confectionery paste made of ground sesame seeds and nuts. She decorated the halvah with chocolate and mixed nuts. Guests ooh'd and ah'd at its unusual taste. Some even had the *chutzpah* to fill their napkins with extra cakes to take home. In a sense, it was a great compliment for Jessie.

Our children stood behind the sweet table and helped serve everything, and in other ways assisted us with the party. Our crew was always the first to arrive at these functions and the last to leave. Several cars were used to transport silver trays and platters, sweets and decorations, and most of it had to be re-packed when we left. We could never have imagined that running a party was so involved. We were busy from the time clients chose their wedding invitations, paper goods, location cards, napkins, orchestra, and the theme of the party, through the throwing of the bride's bouquet and other emcee duties, to the final packing up of leftover wedding cake for the families. We also arranged special lyrics and music for the bride, groom and the parents from both sides of the family, with toasts and the like.

We had to be innovators to find new ways to liven up a party. At many weddings, we included strolling musicians during dinner. Mimicking our *shtick* was the greatest compliment we could receive. As other consultants copied us, we had to keep coming up with new ideas to keep ahead of the competition.

Amidst everything that was going on with our party business, and unbeknownst to me, I was being scouted by a cruise ship agent looking for new acts. I knew it didn't happen by accident. When the agent called me, I asked him how he found out about me. He said, "One of our comedy stars was in one of your revues and recommended you very highly." He then wanted to know where he could hear me sing. Fortunately, on the weekend he was in Chicago, I had a prime show scheduled at the Conrad Hilton in the Loop, for a large cancer organization.

I had appeared in the large Hilton ballroom many times and I was familiar with their set-up. Their mammoth stage had enough room for my 15-piece orchestra, and then some. They were well-equipped with microphones, spotlights, and a fantastic sound system. Fifteen hundred people sitting at round dinner tables was a snap for the hotel.

I relished performing for large organizations that did things in a very professional manner. I knew I would benefit from the Hilton crew making my show as outstanding as possible. Of course, it didn't hurt that I always showed my appreciation to the light and sound men, by getting the organizations to tip them properly.

I was excited about the prospect of doing some cruise shows, because I had heard glowing reports from performers about the fun they had doing them. They had captive audiences ready at all times to enjoy the shows, dancing, gambling, and all the amenities to make passengers happy. Cruise entertainers called it, "a floating paradise." I arranged a special table and dinner for the cruise agent.

Applaudience: The Autobiography of Dale Lind

Jessie and Dale on cruise ship, 1985

When my Hilton show was over, the agent approached me immediately and said, "Where can we talk?" I led him into a side room. He told me that he was quite impressed with my performance, and compared me to John Raitt, the musical comedy star. He offered me a contract for two weeks, with a top salary and a suite for two. I told him I would let him know in a few hours, as soon as I checked with Jessie.

When I got home and told Jess about the offer, she agreed with me that it was too good a deal to pass up and an offer I couldn't refuse! Jessie would be able to spend only the first week with me. She would fly home the second week to prepare for a party we were doing the following weekend. I would return just in time to entertain at the party. My contract called for me to sing on "The Carnival" for the first week, and then transfer to "The Viking" for the second week. We were to be flown from Chicago to Venezuela, where a room was reserved for us at a local hotel. In the morning we would join our ship.

When we arrived in Venezuela, a driver was waiting to take us to the hotel, along with two other acts who would be performing on the same ship. With so much in common, we hit it off and became friends almost immediately. When we reached the hotel, we were dog-tired. The hour was late, the air was tropically hot and muggy, and we were anxious to get to sleep. When we reached our room, it was a joke! There was no air-conditioning, and with the windows open it was exceedingly damp. When we checked the bed, that was an even bigger joke! The mattress was old and lumpy. There was no way we could possibly sleep in that bed.

When I called down to the clerk for a change of rooms, he said they were full up—the usual reply. We had to make the best of it, and decided to put the mattress on the hard floor. We shed our clothing and slept in the nude to keep cool. After five hours of sleeping like the dead, we got our wake-up call, ate a quick breakfast, and left for our ship, thinking, "What a lousy way to start a cruise."

When we arrived at the dock, Jessie and I were overwhelmed as we saw our giant ship painted in white and blue, with hundreds of people looking out at us from three decks. It was a fascinating sight which made us feel so much better. Once aboard, our cabin and surroundings were breathtakingly luxurious.

My contract with "Carnival" stipulated conditions easily met. Our rooms were first-class accommodations, and I was to do only four shows a week. Actually, I worked only two nights a week, doing two shows on each night of performance. That gave us most evenings, and all of our days, to enjoy everything on board and the trips to the islands where the ship put into port.

As soon as we changed our clothes I was paged on our room speaker to attend rehearsal in the show club. We unloaded our bags quickly. I was so delighted with our accommodations that I didn't mind having to rehearse, even though I was dead tired!

When I reached the show room, one of the acts was already rehearsing. I was informed that my first two shows would take place that same night. Everything was happening so fast and I thought, "Hey, that's show business." The real fun began when I handed the orchestra conductor my music. I suddenly realized it was an all-Latino band. When I showed them my music I became aware that none of the musicians spoke a word of English. How in the world would I be able to convey what I wanted? I had special arrangements in special keys which were not the norm, except for show-orchestras that had the necessary experience. But this band had to do triple duty: they played for the cocktail hour, for dancing, and for the shows. Unusual orchestrations were a real challenge! I resorted to all kinds of *shtick* to make myself understood, and when my rehearsal time was up (we were on a short schedule), I figured I would just keep my fingers crossed.

When show time arrived, the other two acts were slated to precede me. Their music was simple and easy for the band to play. When they finished their routines, they received a great hand, and then it was my turn. When the emcee announced my name, I walked down the aisle to the microphone on stage, while the band started playing my introduction. I never expected what I heard! The musicians were so nervous about playing my music that they rushed the opening tempo to three times as fast as we had rehearsed it. There was no way I could possibly sing it at that pace. I stopped the music and said, "Whoa, whoa! Let's start again and do it the way we rehearsed it." My opening song was "When You're Smiling," so I smiled as I tapped out the beat with my hands and feet. By this time, the audience thought I was a comedian and that it was all part of my act. They began to giggle and I went along with it, giggling with them. Finally, the band got it right, and I was on my way.

At least, I thought so until I went into my second song. Suddenly our ship hit some rocky waters and began moving from side to side. As a result, I could hardly keep my feet solidly on the floor. I joked about it to the audience, then I thought quickly and took the mike off the stand. I moved with the ship as I sang my favorite songs: the French "Dites-Moi" from "South Pacific," a medley from "Oklahoma," my Italian version of "Sorrento," and "McNamara's Band." It worked better than I expected. From that time on, wherever I performed I moved constantly with my mike, close to the crowd for a more intimate performance.

Entertaining on that cruise had started as a "comedy of errors," but I persevered. I think about it often now, and I laugh again and again about the whole hilarious episode. It was truly a remarkable two weeks and as the comedians put it, a real gas!

Chapter 44

A Harrowing Experience

One Monday in June, when I said, "Good morning" to Jessie, my voice sounded funny. I had sung at several functions the day before so I thought I must be tired after so much talking and singing. I figured I better not sing for a few days.

Two days later, when I was in the shower, where I love to sing because of the wonderful acoustics, my voice did not respond at all. It had shut down completely. Now I began to get antsy. I tried once more, and the sound that emanated from my throat was cracking and quivering.

I knew it wasn't laryngitis because my speaking voice was still fine. I wasn't ill. I didn't have a cold. I had never had that kind of experience, and I was non-plussed as to what the problem was.

I hurried to my desk, grabbed the phone book, and began to search for throat doctors. I made appointment with two of them so I could compare the diagnosis of one with the other.

After their examinations, neither of them could figure out why my speaking voice functioned and my singing voice didn't. Their advice to me didn't seem right, either. One said, "Do not sing for six months," and the other said, "Maybe it's your hiatal hernia. Try sleeping on several high pillows." I was not impressed. I was certain they were both wrong. I visited two more doctors, and they were more confused than the first two.

Then I remembered a Dr. Katz whom I had gone to some years earlier for hoarseness. He knew I was a cantor and had been as concerned as I was.

After examining me, he said, "Cantor, as far as I am concerned, there is only one doctor in Chicago who can properly diagnose your condition. The fact is, he worked his way through college as a professional singer and understands the vocal condition. He treats opera singers and is given grants by the government for the best equipment necessary for diagnosing all kinds of throat and vocal problems." His name was Dr. Robert Bastian, and he as also an Assistant Professor of Laryngology at Chicago's Loyola University.

I made an appointment with him immediately, and when I met him at Loyola, I was shocked at how young he was. After I told him my problem, he said, "Come with me." He led me into a special room that looked like a lab, and I was amazed at all his equipment and video machines. He asked me to sing certain sounds so he could hear what was wrong. It was worse than ever; I squawked like a chicken. He put me in a position where he could probe my throat with a certain instrument while I watched it all on a video screen. It was fascinating! As he probed, he had me sing again and showed me a part of my vocal chords which was supposed to move as I sang, but which was not functioning.

When the exam was over, he said to me, "Dale, you're going to have to start from scratch like a beginner who is just learning how to sing. You must try to bring back the voice one note at a time without straining. You should start by vocalizing three minutes the first day and increase the time as you go along. You will know what to do as you redevelop each note and keep adding to the scale. It won't be easy, but with your training and experience, you should be able to sing again."

Unfortunately, he could not tell me how long it would take. The High Holidays were only ten weeks away. I knew it would be a Herculean effort to be ready in time. Nobody could do it for me. I would have to sweat it through myself in the short time I had left. Naturally, the whole situation was harrowing. I couldn't sleep, and the worrying didn't help.

Meanwhile, my congregants were reserving their seats and it looked like a sell-out. I discussed with Cary that it would be prudent to teach some of our soloists portions of the solos that I normally did with the choir. Three weeks later, as I struggled with the vocal exercises, I thought it might be a good idea also to hire an assistant cantor—just in case I needed help. I began doing research and found that there was absolutely no one available. The time was too short.

I began making some real progress, and the middle of my range was returning. Now there were only four weeks left, and I forced myself to stay calm and have faith. At choir rehearsals, I stayed mum and just listened. I didn't dare risk any more damage.

With one week left, my falsetto came back, and my high notes began functioning. Still, I took it easy and did not reach for the moon. I had to be very careful and not overdo it.

When Rosh Hashonah Eve finally arrived, only the family, the choir, and a few others knew what I had gone through. Jessie kissed me and kicked me in the tush as she always did to wish me luck before any performance. My soprano soloist, Kati Olsen, who had been with me for over 15 years, said to me, "I'm not worried about you. When you approach your microphone, and see all those people waiting to hear you, you're going to come through like the old pro that you are." It meant a lot to me to know the faith that she had in me.

As I donned my robe and yarmulke, I sent for the sound man. I told him to keep the volume up so I would not have to strain. He assured me he would use good judgment as he always did for everybody involved.

I made the prayer over my cantorial tallis, adorned with silver and gold metallic threads, kissed it as custom required, put it on, and headed for the pulpit. As I entered the sanctuary, there was the usual buzz in the congregation. Then the choir joined me in their royal blue robes, and Cary entered in his white robe and ascended the step up to his conductor's platform. He looked at me with a smile, and nodded to the choir to prepare for the opening prayer.

There was a hush in the congregation as I started my solo. Then the choir followed with the triumphant beginning of the Hebrew *"Ma Tovu,"* "How goodly are thy tents, oh Jacob." We were off and running with everyone beaming. Being on the pulpit and chanting before the altar of God always inspired me and gave me the impetus I needed to give my all.

The choir had practiced many of the numbers in lower keys so that I would not have to strain my voice, especially at the beginning. But Kati proved right, because as I warmed up, I motioned to Cary to raise the pitch

Back row, middle: Michael Cancilla, Dale and son Cary, Kati Olsen and nephew Steven Platt behind Cary; middle row: sisters Selma and Norma at right end; front row: granddaughters Joanna and Allison, nieces Donna Platt and Mary Beth Crum.

so our music would sound as brilliant as it always did. We could see that the lower voices were delighted to "come out of the basement."

I was extremely grateful to everybody on the pulpit who had been so supportive during my agony and trepidation, and I appreciated Dr. Bastian for his knowledge in giving me the right advice. It had taken my greatest effort and discipline to recover my voice, but in the end I was able to come through for my congregation. For the first time in many months, I felt whole again.

Chapter 45

THE HOLY LAND OF OUR ANCESTORS

At this juncture of our lives, Jessie and I decided it was the right time to visit the Holy Land of our forefathers. It was the 70s, and Israel was flourishing. One million Arabs were working with the labor force in Israel. They, too, were enjoying Israel's prosperity and innovations. We had heard about the many miracles that Israeli scientists and engineers were performing, and we had to see for ourselves the wonders they had created.

We joined a small tour of a Chicago chapter of Women's American ORT, for which Jessie had worked so hard as President for so many years. After getting our passports, we were off to the "Land of Milk and Honey." During our long plane ride, the excitement of passengers and their chattering was endless. Sleep was difficult, and the flight attendants were constantly busy.

ORT's mission was always to rehabilitate and train people for jobs and opportunities. We were to be given a special tour of Israel, including seeing the location where planes and armor were being built underground. There were other revelations as well.

After hours and hours in the air, the captain finally announced that we would arrive in Tel Aviv in fifteen minutes. Everyone applauded. The emotional impact was stunning, as everyone sat up and looked out of their windows at the roof-tops of thousands of homes and buildings. My heart was racing a mile a minute!

As we landed, music and singing was coming from everywhere. "*Hatikvah*" ("The Hope"—the national anthem of Israel), "*Heveinu*

Shalom Aleichem" ("We Have Brought You Peace"), and other Israeli songs blared from loudspeakers. It was bedlam as we emerged from the plane where dignitaries, families, and friends were waiting to greet passengers. What a thrilling way for us to begin our sojourn. There were tears galore, and some people kissed the holy ground. The whole atmosphere was charged with such emotion that it was almost unbearable.

For most of my life, beginning from my childhood cantorial days, I had chanted the Yom Kippur Neelah, the culminating service, which closes with the words *"Leshono habo birusholayim,"* "Next year in Jerusalem." Now it was a reality and my heart almost burst with joy!

When we arrived at the King David hotel, people were huddled together at the reservation desk. Others were sitting around speaking Yiddish, Hebrew, and other foreign languages. As we watched Arabs and other people wearing their native garb, including Indians in their saris, we realized that not only was Israel the only democracy in the Middle East, but it had become a melting pot of all races, creeds, and colors. The fact that Arabs and Jews worship the same prophets, Abraham, David, and Moses, makes the continuing conflict between them shocking and stupid. How sad!

As we stood in the lobby waiting for our rooms, a voice suddenly rang out, "Dale Lind—thank God you are here." It was Rabbi William Novick, the head of the Weitzman Institute. He went on to tell me that Jan Peerce, the international opera star, was supposed to make the Kiddush at their special Shabbos dinner taking place that evening. Peerce had taken ill, and had to cancel his flight from New York. Rabbi Novick asked that I take his place. My reputation had preceded me even in Israel.

I was delighted by his request, and also complimented to be asked to replace Peerce. But I was so tired from the trip that I wondered if I could sing at all. There would be no time to vocalize and perk myself up. I accepted, hoping that just being there was dramatic enough to provide the adrenaline I needed.

Jessie suggested that we go to our room and rest. She was absolutely right. I rested and felt better, but I couldn't sleep. After all, I was going to sing my first song in Israel. Wow! What a thrill to sing in the Holy Land. It reminded me of the time when my parents traveled to Israel, in 1950, to see for themselves the wonder of our state. Peerce was a student of my dad's, and oddly enough was also in Israel at the same time. When he heard that Joshua Lind was in Israel, Peerce notified the proper authorities to pressure my father into doing Sabbath services in Jerusalem as a guest cantor.

My father was so honored, and filled with such profound emotion and anticipation, that he couldn't wait to pour his heart out on the designated pulpit. When Israeli radio announced Dad's guest appearance, the general public reacted by packing the congregation. Jews dressed in their Sabbath fineries anxiously waited and wondered, "What was Joshua Lind like?" Later, Dad told our family that as he ascended the pulpit surrounded by ultra-orthodox worshippers, his heart was in his mouth. As he began chanting the opening prayer *"Lechu-neranenu,"* he calmed himself by slowly warming up his voice. Little by little, like vocalizing at home, he started using more volume. In his early years in New York City, Dad had studied with the famed opera teacher, "Roxis." Now his training came to bear. As he opened up his dramatic tenor voice, which rang with poignancy, he could see that the congregants were moved. As Dad progressed with the services, he could feel the impact he was creating.

By the time he finished the services, the worshippers were on such an emotional high that they literally carried him from the pulpit yelling accolades in Hebrew. They blessed him with *"Yasher koach!"* "Strength unto you!" Dad told us that tears started flowing down his face. He was so touched with the honors bestowed upon him that it became a highlight of his life. How could he ever forget that he had chanted on a holy pulpit in Israel—the sacred land of our ancestors?

Now it was *my* turn to perform in Israel. When I began the Kiddush wine service, I gave it all the power I could muster. As I chanted, I was so emotional, like my Dad before me, that my heart was singing, not just my voice. When I finished, they gave me a wonderful reception, which set me up for the rest of our tour.

Touring the hot spots of Tel Aviv reminded me of a little New York: the hustle and bustle and sheer volume of cabs, busses, and people in the crowded streets was similar. Cigarette butts and newspapers were strewn all over the downtown area. The loud, brash, neon signs in large letters advertising American products, along with numerous restaurants, newspaper stands, and movie houses, reminded me of Broadway and 42nd Street when I was a youngster. As we ventured down Diegendoff Street, with outside dining where people talked and smoked like crazy, I mused that this was not the Holy Land we had anticipated!

What shocked me was being surrounded by soldiers with rifles strapped on their shoulders. Seeing young, beautiful, female *sabras* (native-born Israelis) in uniform, keeping the peace and ready to fight or quell riots alongside the male soldiers, was an awesome sight. Male soldiers were unusually tall and handsome, while the female soldiers, with their dark features mid-Eastern good looks, were absolutely striking.

I thought of our ancestors who dreamed and prayed for two thousand years for our own Homeland. We were so lucky to be there in the flesh—to see for ourselves the fulfillment of the prophecy. I thought, "Are we really here?"

Our Israeli tour guide took us everywhere and explained the history of Israel, its architecture and archeological sights, things we never knew existed. We visited the beautiful city of Haifa, with its hills and valleys. We spent time on *Kibbutzim*, communal farms, and saw with our own eyes the fruits of their labors. Wherever we went with our bus—for miles and miles—we saw trees with thousands of water sprinklers spouting. The irrigation and surrounding landscape was magnificent. A whole new world had opened up to us. The only shame of it all was that all bus drivers had to keep rifles nearby—just in case. That is the fear they live with every day.

One of our special treats was to visit Jaffa at night. There were street vendors selling knick-knacks and souvenirs. There were also art stores and all kinds of shops. The streets were so lively with people of every ilk, that again I felt like I was in New York City. Our special thrill in Jaffa was attending a nightclub to hear a native entertainer. A famous recording artist, Chava Alberstein, was the featured star. She was absolutely delightful in her presentation of Israeli songs. When her performance was over, the pianist, who was also the M.C. and owner of the club, was handed a note by one of the waiters. After he read the note, he announced: "I understand that we have a famous Chicago entertainer in the room, Dale Lind. Would you please come up and favor us with a song?" Obviously, one of our tour members revealed my presence.

I couldn't refuse to perform, because everyone started yelling my name.

As I made my way to the stage I said to the pianist, "I don't have any music with me." He assured me he could accompany me with whatever I chose. So I said, "How about "Rumania, Rumania"? I launched into the song and finished to cheers of "More! More!" I made an instant decision.

I said to the M.C., "I'd like to do a duet with your entertainer, Chava." He yelled for her, and she obliged.

As she joined me, she said, "What should we sing?" At that time "Jerusalem of Gold" was the most popular song in Israel. I suggested to Chava that we try that one. Well, it was a show-stopper and a special thrill for me, for Jessie, and for everyone present. It was another wonderful memory to store away with so many yet to come. We should have taken pictures!

The next day we toured the streets of Mir-Hashirim, in Jerusalem, a street that was extraordinary to behold. Jewish merchants sold religious artifacts such as: *taleisim* (fringed prayer shawls), *mezuzas, menorahs* (candleholders for the holiday of *Chanukah*), and every conceivable item prevalent in a Jewish household. On Fridays, merchants close their shops in early afternoon to prepare for the Holy Sabbath. No vehicles are allowed on the streets until the Sabbath is over.

We made trips to Safed and Caesaria. In Safed, we walked through an entire area of artists who were sculpting, drawing, and painting canvasses. We felt it a privilege to buy some of their works, so we could adorn our walls at home.

Caesaria was a phenomenal experience! It was 9:00 A.M. when we arrived at a sight we couldn't believe. It was an open-air arena that sunk down many feet to its center-stage. Dug up by archaeologists, the marble and concrete seating was just as it was thousands of years ago. It was actually a theatre in the round. I was curious and had to go down to the bottom of the arena to see what it felt like. As I stood there in the center, our guide yelled down to me, "You have to sing something!" When the rest of the tour chimed in, I agreed—reluctantly.

I thought, "Holy Moses, it's only 9:00 A.M. I'm not awake yet!" I decided to sing, "My Yiddishe Mame." The acoustics were naturally great and sounded like I had been singing through a sound system. My voice was amplified by nature's surroundings. While I was singing, other visitors in the surrounding area sat down to listen, and the arena filled up quickly. By the time I was through, applause boomed out. The whole experience was astounding. Chalk up another inspiring memory!

It was a real stroke of luck when we met Dr. Imber of Chicago in the lobby of our hotel. Dr. Imber always held high positions in world-wide *B'nai B'rith* Councils, and in the Anti-Defamation League. This time he was in Israel as a delegate to their International Convention. When he recognized me, he greeted me with his warm smile and asked if Jessie and I would like to hear Golda Meir speak at the convention. I responded with, "Would I!" But then I told him we were with a tour of ten people from ORT.

Dr. Imber said, "Bring them all," and then handed me tickets for the whole group. How magnanimous! And what a treasure we were about to see.

As we sat in a large auditorium in Tel Aviv, speakers from many parts of the world ascended to the podium and said their piece. Some were great orators and spoke about the purpose of *B'Nai Brith,* while others spoke about the importance of Israel.

When Golda Meir was finally called to the dais, the whole assembly stood up and gave her a tremendous ovation! I wondered, "How in the world can she follow all those fabulous speakers?" I needn't have worried. As she walked to the lectern, wearing her health shoes, and began to speak, there was an aura around this frail little grandma, and a charisma that was so powerful that we all sat there mesmerized, in hushed silence. As she expounded on her work, and poured out her deepest emotions about the State of Israel, we forgot completely about the other speakers. Her dynamic oratory for ninety minutes—without notes, speaking extemporaneously—was the most stunning speech I had ever heard. We were all touched beyond words. Now we knew why she had been elected Prime Minister and why she gave up her personal life in Wisconsin. It was total devotion and dedication to our Jewish Homeland. What a night and what a thrill to have been in her presence.

There was a story about Golda, when she went to the doctor for her annual check-up. She smoked cigarette after cigarette. Finally, the doctor said, "Golda, you shouldn't be smoking so much. It's bad for your health." Golda looked at him, smiled, and said, "For the few years I have left, I might as well enjoy myself." She was known for her great sense of humor. During her speech, she told of a visitor who had approached her and asked, "Madam Prime Minister, so many of us are wondering how in the world you defeated the Arab armies and their back-up of two million Arabs in five wars in such a short time?"

"Well," she answered, "Fortunately, my strategy worked. I just put the doctors and accountants in the front line, and boy, can they CHARGE!"

There were other unique events during our trip, like climbing to the top of the Masada and witnessing from its peak, the exact same surroundings that a handful of Jews had witnessed for months, as they held off the Roman Army during the first century of the Common Era. When the Roman soldiers, after many attacks, finally made it to the top of the Masada, the Jews decided that committing mass suicide was their only option to escape the wrath of the Romans. Now, the same Masada is where thousands of parents and their 12 and 13-year-old children make their trek from America and from all over the world, to celebrate their Bar and Bat Mitzvah rituals. What a great way to experience the history of our forefathers.

In Israel, children of that age are already doing adults' work—making airplane motors along with other components for defense purposes. I remember it as one of the most fascinating sights we had ever seen. It seemed unreal—like we were watching a movie unfolding before us. Can you imagine seeing young children working with adults in building Israeli defense systems? The children, some as young as twelve, were being taught everything about the inner workings of Israeli military equipment. This new generation of children was being educated as engineers, scientists, mathematicians, and teachers who eventually would run the State of Israel. We were so proud of them, but careful not to reveal the things we saw to the rest of the world. It was "hush-hush!" How fortunate we are that our American kids do not have to do the things children must do in Israel to stay safe and preserve their freedom. American children take freedom for granted.

Touring the Yad-Vashem Museum in Israel was the most heartbreaking experience of all. We looked at horrific pictures of Holocaust victims, and were reminded of the crematoria and the loss of so many loved ones. We, and all the members of our tour, shed buckets of tears, and repeated over and over, "Never, Never, Never Again!"

Flying back to Chicago, Jessie and I talked incessantly about all the things we had seen and the amazing events we had witnessed. When we landed in Chicago, we were on a "high," and didn't come back to reality for weeks. When we eventually returned to our daily lives, it all seemed like a dream! We realized how fortunate we were to have walked on the same sacred land as our Prophets and ancestors did thousands of years ago, and hoped to do so some day again.

Chapter 46

A New Generation

Membership in our congregation was growing faster than we anticipated. Obviously, the Jewish community had accepted me not only as a clergyman, but also as a true minister of my own congregation. I had decided that my first priority would be to fulfill the needs of our congregants, who now looked to me to conduct their weddings and other religious functions. In many ways, I had become their counselor and psychiatrist, as we shared their celebrations and listened to their problems.

When brides and grooms entered my study for premarital counseling, it was only natural that a closeness would develop between their families and ours. It therefore came as a shocking revelation to me when youngsters I had known as children, began living with their future spouses before marriage. Parents were beside themselves, especially when their children asked to share their bedrooms at home with their boyfriends or girlfriends. The "oy-vays," and the wringing of hands went on for quite some time. Kids were meeting other kids of different faiths at school or at work and falling in love. Sometimes their relationships fell apart, and other times it led to marriage. Finding a clergyman to marry them was almost impossible, as men of the clergy stuck to the old rules and traditions of their faiths. Brides and grooms of mixed marriages, not wanting to offend their families with a church or synagogue atmosphere, were scrambling to find a neutral choice. Usually they ended up in a hotel ballroom, with all the trimmings of a chapel: candles, flowers, and other appropriate adornments.

I was one of the first Jewish clergymen to face the challenge of performing an interfaith wedding. It all started when my nephew Brian decided to marry Laura, his Catholic girlfriend. When they asked me to co-perform their ceremony with a friend of Laura's who was a priest, I struggled with myself and my conscience as to whether I should do it. Then I thought, if a priest could accept the situation, how could I take a prejudicial stance against it? Besides, it was my sister Selma's son. How could I possibly disappoint her? I wondered what to eliminate from my regular wedding service, and what I could say to make this mixed situation palatable. I pondered about it for days.

I also thought about our prophet Moses, to whom God spoke and delivered the Ten Commandments, which was the beginning of all law. Moses, who freed our people from slavery, also married out of the faith when he chose Zipporah from Midian, who eventually converted to Judaism. Then there was Esther who married Achashveirosh, a king and a non-Jew. It was she who alerted her husband about Haman's plot to destroy the Jews .The King, in turn, destroyed Haman.

When I spoke to Brian and Laura, I could feel the love they had for each other, and I thought "Dear God, tell me what to do." My answer came quickly as I said "yes" to performing the wedding. Selma, Brian and Laura were so happy with my decision. Now, I had to figure out what to say at the ceremony, and how to participate with a priest. I knew there would be nothing wrong with making some blessings over the wine and breaking the traditional glass. There would be a canopy, too. I could explain all of the symbols, and say some meaningful words that would bring everyone together, no matter what their faith. I remembered a poem that I repeated at the ceremony which proclaimed:

> Tear down the walls,
> God made of one all men who live upon the Earth.
> He is our Father
> and we his children, no matter what our human birth,
> Tear down the walls that separate,
> and breed estrangement, pride and hate,
> The poor, the oppressed, the rich and the great
> are all really brothers in one human estate.

Performing Brian and Laura's wedding was a milestone for me. When I saw how pleased everyone was—that two people from such different backgrounds and faiths, could be married in a warm loving way, I realized that I had done the right thing. I decided that I would continue to join couples in this new kind of union. I felt it was time to help end so much bigotry in the world, and bring people together.

When word got around that I was performing mixed marriages, I was besieged with phone calls, especially from Jewish parents delighted to have someone they knew marry their children. Of course, there were the usual dissenters and the "holier-than-thou" people who raged against me. Then I heard that there were some Reform rabbis who could not refuse their own parishioners with the same problem. They, too, got flack from other temple members.

As the years went by, objections lessened because so many families were going through the same situation. There was an avalanche of young people turning away from those of their own faith, and not because they didn't want to continue in their own religion. They just found what they desired in someone outside of their own faith. Love was always uppermost!

I thought of all the fruitless wars that are still on-going because of religious differences, and because people worshiped Gods with different names. Now, with so many mixed marriages, our young people seemed to be saying to their elders, "We're all God's children." Why not set an example for a greater brotherhood?

It is interesting to note an important passage in the *Haggadah*, a special pamphlet which tells the Passover story of the Jewish exodus from Egypt. As Moses parted the waters of the Red Sea and led the Israelites to freedom on the other side, Pharoah's armies began to pursue them. The Israelites were frantic and began screaming. When Moses raised his wand and the waters came together, drowning the Egyptians, the Israelites rejoiced, yelling and dancing. At that moment, Moses heard the voice of God, saying, "How can you rejoice when my children are dying?"

Today, in Israel, Jews and Arabs who worship the same prophets and are really cousins—descendants from Abraham—are still at war with each other. When will the stupidity of it all end? Believing in different faiths should not be a criterion to destroy each other. I find that most young people about to marry really want the same things: someone to love, a measure of success, good health, and the joy of life. Yet leaders of different sects and religions constantly fight among themselves for the power to rule in domains around the world. It's pure insanity!

I have always felt strongly about the commandment "Love Thy Neighbor as Thyself." Born and created in His image, it is incumbent upon us to adhere to that commandment, so brotherhood between faiths can become a reality in our time. It seems to me that as parents, we have a duty to teach our children *tolerance*. Living in a world of so many different religions, we must respect the faith of others as they perceive it. We cannot live in a cocoon any more. If there are those of our children who can commit to a deep and abiding love—the most powerful emotion they can possibly feel for another human being—then who are we to say, "It is not the way."

Let us remember that it was the Lord, Himself, who spoke to Moses as He forged the ten commandments, commanding us to "love our neighbors" no matter who they are. There is an eternal wisdom in that, which, if followed, will bring humankind together as all of us seek a greater understanding of all God's children.

Chapter 47

STUNNING FAMILY MEMORIES

We were so proud when Cary graduated from Brandeis University, and then law school at Northwestern University. When he came to our home with his girl friend, Sandy Spellman, to inform us that they wanted to get married, we were ecstatic! As party consultants, we had always been involved with other people's celebrations. Now, we could enjoy our own supreme moment and our own *simcha*! It was especially great because we had known Sandy's parents for quite some years. Her mother, Phyllis, a charming and vivacious person, had sung in my choir, and we looked forward to being *machatonim*, related through marriage. The wedding was great fun. The band was superb and for the Lind family it was as the song goes, "A Grand Night For Singing."

After a few years, Cary opened his own law practice, while Barbara was singing in orchestra and opera company choruses, as well as teaching voice to many students in her own home studio. With the kids now so grown up, I was beginning to feel my age until Cary and Sandy, in the ensuing years, presented us with two beautiful grandchildren. With Joanna and Allison joining our family, Jessie and I felt reinvigorated as grandparents.

As soon as our granddaughters reached the age of five, they became soloists in my choir. They sang the same solos Barbara and Cary had sung so many years before. Members of my congregation couldn't wait for the High Holy Days, so they could hear the two sisters sing. It touched our hearts when the family of one of our members who was deathly ill told us that his one wish was to hear *"die klayne maydelech"* (the little girls) sing again. The girls were so popular that the rest of us took a back seat,

Dale with granddaughters Joanna & Allison, High Holidays, 1989

even though I featured an unbelievable operatic coloratura soprano along with other fabulous soloists, accompanied by a symphonic choir of twenty-four great voices.

I not only composed solos and duets for our girls, but I felt inspired to present something even more spectacular. I began with a few trios in which Cary and I took turns singing with the kids. Then came the *pièce de resistance:* I wrote some quartets that would feature the girls, myself, and Cary, who would leave the podium from which he conducted the choir, and join us at the microphones. The results were ethereal and heavenly. No one had ever heard two sisters singing with their father and grandfather at the same time. We had made cantorial history—a first in synagogue music which I think will never be repeated.

Joanna and Allison were following in the footsteps of Cary and Barbara, both on stage and on the synagogue pulpit. Then our grandkids decided to go a bit further, joining the Lyric Opera Children's Chorus and the Chicago Opera Theatre. They were also chosen as soloists: Allison was the voice of the shepherd in "Fedora," which starred Placido Domingo and Mirella Freni, while Joanna was one of three Spirits in "The Magic Flute." I guess it's in the genes. Again and again, I have repeated to Jessie, "My God, look what we started. Aren't you proud?"

Running my own congregation allowed me many titles. I was referred to as Reverend, Cantor, and Rabbi. The fact that I had been doing double duty as cantor and rabbi, sermonizing and chanting, led to the varied titles. My dear father, Joshua, had wisely prepared me for all clergy duties by insisting that I go through religious training at New York City's *Yitzchok-Alchonin Yeshiva*. It was all so many years ago, but now served my purpose in every way.

When the world-famous operatic tenor and cantor, Richard Tucker, died, his synagogue went into mourning. The Park Synagogue in Chicago's Loop had been founded on Tucker's reputation, and now that he was gone, his synagogue was in deep trouble financially. The board of directors got in touch with me to ask if I would consider the cantorial position and integrate my congregation with theirs. They made me a very lucrative offer which I was forced to turn down. Most of my members lived on the far North Side, and I could never take on the responsibility of bringing my congregation to a Loop location. It just wasn't feasible. Also, there was no way I would want their Board of Directors telling me how to run my services. I had gone through that many times, and I had promised myself and Jessie, "Never again." Nothing could convince me to change the status I had spent years to attain.

As it happened, instead of moving my congregation to The Park Synagogue, a whole new cadre of Tucker's members joined us at *B'Nai Joshua*. Two of their distinguished members were tireless workers: Floyd and Brana Blatt. I decided to ask Floyd to take over many of the duties on our pulpit. He had been President of Tucker's synagogue for years and was by nature a dedicated leader, sincere and knowledgeable in congregation activities.

Floyd had been a professional trumpet player before becoming an industrialist. When I asked him if he would sound the *shofar*, a ram's horn blown during New Year services, he was delighted. The shofar he would be using had been presented to us from the State of Israel, for raising a great deal of money with our Israel bond drives. Floyd was thrilled to use a *shofar* from the Holy Land, regarding it as a special privilege and personal blessing.

When the congregation heard him sound the *shofar* for the first time, they were shocked. I uttered the tekiyas which precede the *shofar*, and Floyd answered with the traditional short blasts and staccato sounds. At the end of the prayer, the final note is held for as long as the *shofar* blower can manage. After I chanted the last *tekiya*, Floyd amazed all of us, holding the final note endlessly. There were "wows" and "murmurs" in the congregation and the choir. A great *shofar*-sounder had been the one missing element in our service. Fate had brought us a gem. Floyd thrilled all of us no end, and I felt lucky to have him as a leader and friend.

After seven wonderful years at the Orrington, we were shocked when the management informed us that our services could no longer take place at their hotel. A group of investors had purchased the hotel and were set to remodel all the rooms, the lobbies, and banquet rooms. The hotel would be shuttered for several years as the multi-million dollar project would begin. We were saddened to lose our space. This time Fate had dealt us a low blow!

Evanston was overcrowded, which prompted us to widen our search to the entire North Shore area. After some months, we found a facility in Morton Grove, The Fireside Inn. When we sought out the owners we found that they needed us as much as we needed them. They needed the exposure we could provide, and we needed the space that they could provide. While rental fees would exceed what we were paying the Orrington Hotel, we had no alternative but to except their terms.

As soon as we began our ad campaign, the trouble-makers were at it again! They ran to the Fireside, entered the owners' offices, and demanded that they cancel our arrangements. The non-Jewish owners were so shocked at their "*chutzpah*" that they ordered them out immediately, threatening to call the police.

When I told Floyd what had happened, he was enraged. He said, "Dale, you stay out of it. I'm going to handle this whole thing." He then wrote them the most stinging letter any synagogue president could ever have written. He berated them and told them to look to their own services, that if they were losing members, then obviously they were not doing things right. He said that I was fulfilling their religious needs, and they had no right to infringe on our religious institution. After some weeks went by with no reply, I knew in my bones that they were thinking up some other tactic to aggravate me. I was right!

Just as we began setting up the aisles and seating, the Morton Grove Fire Department showed up. They cited all kinds of rules like roping the seats together (a long and tedious job), having much wider aisles, and limiting our seating capacity. We knew who was responsible. It was so obvious. We did everything the Fire Marshall demanded, and when the inspectors revisited our ballroom, everything was in place. That ended the harassment for the next 18 years.

Some years later, when Floyd and Brana retired to Florida, their son, Jeffrey, came to our rescue and very ably assisted us with the pulpit duties. He practiced sounding the *shofar* and did a creditable job, but never quite like his father.

It was never an easy chore for me to do double duty as Cantor and Rabbi. It meant vocalizing between 6:00 and 9:00 A.M., not an easy task for any singer. While sermonizing, I had to make sure to reserve some of my voice so as to make it through the remainder of the singing. It was always a worry because I demanded so much of myself, and especially for the difficult cantorial solos with the choir. They were a magnificent group of men and women which included my talented sisters, Selma and Norma, along with Norma's three children, Steven, Mary Beth and

Donna, all of whom excelled as singers. Many of my singers were music majors at Northwestern University, and others were with Chicago's Lyric Opera. I found myself doing the same thing my beloved father had done when he hired super-tenor Jan Peerce and other great singers.

As the Cantor, the choir looked to me for inspiration and I had to be in prime voice at all times, as a sort of spark-plug. As choir director, Cary always knew what was needed to create the dramatic effects I always sought with our compositions. That was essential as he conducted tirelessly, coordinating all the elements of a proper cohesion between the choir and myself.

I was so proud of my son for his stamina and professionalism that my gratitude and thanks to him had no bounds. There were times, albeit not too often, when I didn't feel good vocally. Cary and I would have to make some changes in a matter of minutes. He always caught my gist and knew exactly what he had to do to help me make it through. What a blessing to have had him at my side for so many years.

As time went on, I knew I needed someone to ease my pulpit duties. I had to find a dynamic speaker who could mesmerize an audience. He also had to be able to explain certain aspects of the liturgy. Was such a person available? I thought it over for some time, and then it hit me! Why not ask Phil to join me? Who could fill my need better than my brother? He was the most capable person I knew, with a great sense of humor to boot. That was an element he always included in his speeches, and audiences loved him.

Phil had suffered from rheumatoid arthritis for years. He had left Chicago to live in Palm Springs, where he was able to adjust to his condition. I knew he was bored with his life. If he was able in any way to help, it would certainly be a plus for me and a boon to my congregants.

When I asked him if he felt well enough to help me, he was ecstatic, and said, "Dale, just being on the pulpit with you would be the best medicine for my aches and pains. Also, I could be with my kids in Chicago and we could all worship together." I knew Phil loved the stage as I did. It would be great for his ego, too. He could prepare sermons and explanations of the texts, and working together would feel like old times.

When he arrived for the Holidays, I was thrilled! When we walked to the pulpit in our robes, my congregants were overwhelmed to see us together. And when he spoke, my tears began to flow. All our relatives in the choir were overcome with joy.

Chapter 48

A Heart-rending Reunion

After many years with Phil, I got another inspiration. I thought, "Wouldn't it be fantastic if I could get Murray to join us, too?" Murray had lost his wife, Pearl, and was coping with polymyositis, a crippling disease which was slowly deteriorating his muscles. He had remarried and retired to Florida with his new wife, Jeanette. It was a forced retirement, because ascending the pulpit steps, as well as many other obstacles, had become impossible for him. As debilitating as his disease was, his voice was still functioning and he was doing High Holiday services in Florida. Ironically, that engagement ended at the same time I had the idea that he might want to join us. I contacted him about coming to Chicago for the coming holidays. He was very excited at the prospect. I knew that it would prove to be a spectacular event to have all three Lind Brothers together again on the same pulpit. How long it had been! I would not ask him to do too much because his illness was much too severe.

When Murray arrived at my congregation, he could hardly ascend the steps without help. When we met, it was pure emotion as we hugged and kissed. This was a double-edged moment—both sad and joyous. It was tough to see my brother suffering so. And yet, I knew I was doing the right thing. I also felt there would never be another such opportunity. We decided that he should chant one complete service. We chose the *Neelah*, the very poignant service that concludes *Yom Kippur*. This is also the last cantorial service for congregants to remember until the following year.

The choir assisted Murray with the proper refrains as Phil and I sat and listened intently. Murray's performance at that *Neelah* Service can only be described by one word: magnificent! It was such a heart-wrenching performance that the entire assemblage, including the choir and our congregants, were entranced and in admiration of Murray's performance. His chanting came so deeply from his soul that it was as if he was crying out to the Almighty Himself, for healing and forgiveness not only for himself, but for our entire congregation. As Phil and I listened to him singing the melodies my father had taught all of us, our faces were wet with uncontrollable tears.

Murray's praying and chanting with a sick body, his reaching out to the Heavens, was soul singing in its highest form—and glorious to the end! On top of that, it was so emotional and profound for the three of us to be together once again on God's pulpit that we could hardly contain ourselves. When the end came, and we joined together on the closing refrains, we hugged and kissed each other again, knowing in our hearts that this precious moment would never happen again in this life.

Chapter 49

ATONEMENT

In the year 2000, after 27 years of conducting services as the Sons of Joshua Congregation, Jessie and I were thinking about retiring and shutting down the synagogue. So many of our members had moved to warmer climates, while others passed away. We were facing other obstacles, as well, including the loss of some of my prime singers. An inner voice was telling me, "This is the time. You've done well. Quit while you're on top."

When Phil returned to Palm Springs because he was ailing and could hardly stand while delivering his sermons, I had no alternative but to take over. Once more it was double duty for me—chanting and delivering the sermons. I knew now that this would be our final year. My last High Holiday services as Cantor were approaching and I strove to make them special, for us to remember the rest of our lives. It was, therefore, important to me that I deliver my best *Yom Kippur* sermons ever. I pondered over what messages I could give my congregants that would not only be meaningful to them, but to my family as well.

During my lifetime as a clergyman, I had suffered so much animosity, had so many rocks thrown at me, that I had been carrying bitterness in my heart for too long. Even though I had overcome so much, and won the battles I fought, the scars and bad feelings I had towards others were still with me. It was time for me to atone. *Yom Kippur* was always the special day to cleanse our whole selves of hatred, revenge and the rage we feel at times. After much contemplation, I decided to speak about the importance of forgiveness—for myself, and for everyone present in my congregation.

When the eve of *Yom Kippur* arrived, and the choir and I had finished the soulful melodies and familiar strains of the age-old *"Kol Nidre,"* "Our Vows," there was a strange quiet in the air. I had rarely heard my congregation so silent. Obviously the chanting of the *Kol Nidre* had touched them so deeply that they just sat there mesmerized. I was in a sweat, feeling a profound holiness in the atmosphere, as if the angels of God were present and ready to receive our prayers of atonement and hopes for a better New Year.

As I prepared to sermonize, I had mixed feelings. I knew I had to feel my words deeply. They had to come genuinely from my heart, my mind, and my whole being. I had to believe what I would now convey to my congregants, that as we forgive others, God would surely forgive us. Here are my words of that night.

> This is the time of atonement, when we ask Almighty God to forgive us for even the smallest indiscretion, every thoughtless act, whether it be slander or gossip, envy or falsehood, and transgressions we have committed this past year and years gone by. That is what our most sacred *Yom Kippur* represents to all Jewry, as we pray for forgiveness for each and every one of us.
>
> This is no easy task! Many of us say things we are sorry for—too late. Some of us carry grudges for a lifetime and are filled with anger about someone or something that fires up our emotions, creating bitterness and hostility. Little do we realize that these bad feelings are not only a mental and emotional burden that sometimes plagues us for years, but in the opinion of many psychologists, it is the cause of deep-rooted stress and even illness.
>
> For decades, "forgiveness" has been discussed in biblical and theological terms. But now, little by little, doctors are examining more thoroughly the physiology of forgiveness, because they want to determine, once and for all, whether one's ability to forgive reduces stress and prevents all kinds

of health problems. Discussions are now taking place in clinics and seminars throughout the world to understand the human act of forgiveness in all its aspects, and just like prayer and meditation, forgiveness may just turn out to be good medicine.

When we think of the percentage of divorces that are now so dominant in our society, we know that family relationships are being destroyed by unforgiving people. Friendships, too, are falling apart because one or the other refuses to forgive, as human emotions well up in anger, hate and misunderstandings. Forgiveness is an idea whose time has come, because it takes away what comes between your family, your friends, and yourself. Psychologists now recognize that when one forgives, and shakes the hand of his so-called enemy, the misery he has been feeling for too long is suddenly gone, and the quality of life increases for the better. At this time of atonement, it behooves us all to begin the process of healing, with a greater resolve to set aside old grievances, no matter who is to blame and no matter what the reason.

Perhaps we should learn from three remarkable and magnanimous people who exerted their power to forgive, and in turn cleansed their own feelings of anger and revenge. First, I cite Cardinal Bernardin, who forgave the man who falsely accused him of sexual abuse. Second, there is Nelson Mandela, who in 1990 emerged from 27 years in a South African prison, remarkably free from bitterness. Instead of retaliating against those who embraced Apartheid, Mandela set up a commission in an attempt to heal the nation's wounds. And third, there is the New York policeman, Detective Steven McDonald, who forgave the young man whose bullet paralyzed him in 1986. McDonald later became a strong advocate of forgiveness, and even took his message to strife-torn Northern Ireland. It took great courage and grace for them to forgive those who trespassed against them.

There have been many others who have received the ultimate reward of a profound change in their lives for the better, when they showed compassion, wisdom, and the courage to forgive.

There is an old Chinese proverb that says, "A man who opts for revenge may as well dig two graves." Think of it! What a wonderful world this could become if husbands and wives, man and man, nations and nations, would forgive each other for wrongful acts committed against one another. Peace would become a reality, and a great healing would take place in our hearts, our feelings and yes, even in our bodies, as we rid ourselves of the curse of bitterness, rage and stubbornness. It is time to put in the past that which created such grievances, and replace it with a new understanding of what our humanity should be.

Now is the time for us to change, not tomorrow or next year. As we pray tonight and tomorrow, let us cleanse ourselves of hatred and ask the Almighty to forgive our iniquities, as we forgive those who sinned against us. To all who are here tonight, let me hear from all of you a great shout of "Amen!"

Chapter 50

Retirement

We knew that our congregants would not take our retirement too well. First we informed the family and all those who took part in the services, including the choir. Then we notified the congregation with a letter of regret and farewell. It was an especially sad time for our children and grandchildren. It did not surprise me when Cary and Sandy told us that our granddaughters cried when they heard the news. They had been soloing in the choir since they were five and six years old. I was sure that Cary, Sandy and Barbara would understand that retiring from conducting High Holiday Services was inevitable. I would still perform lesser services, such as weddings. My sisters, nieces and nephew had sung in the choir since our first year. They, too, were shocked at our closing, as were all the rest of the family and friends.

I had chanted the High Holy Day services for most of my life. The toughest time for me would be when Jessie and I had to become part of another congregation, with another cantor and choir, probably singing many unfamiliar melodies. All my synagogue music was written by my father and myself. Now it would be different, and we had to accept that. A colleague of mine, Shlomo Shuster, whom I always admired, had been cantor at Niles Township Congregation in Skokie for many years. I decided we would feel most at home with him. Shlomo also shared the pulpit with Rabbi Neil Brief, who co-performed with me at several functions. Knowing both of them so well, I felt confident that we would have a wonderful relationship.

I remembered when the Northwest Council of Synagogues attempted to stop my services, and the only rabbi that encouraged me was Rabbi

Brief. Right after the hullabaloo began, we had met at a theatre and he said to me, "You are doing a great *mitzvah*, a wonderful deed for unaffiliated Jews, by providing them with a place to worship." For having the decency to say what he did, and for welcoming my former congregants to the Niles Township Congregation, I shall always be in his debt.

When many of our former members accepted our invitation to join us there, it softened the sadness we all felt. During the Holy Days we were so warmly greeted by everyone present, that as long as we were together, the spirit of our Sons of Joshua congregation would live forever. The best thing about it all, was that for the first time in our lives, our entire family could sit together in worship, without the stress involved in running an entire congregation.

Chapter 51

GIVING BACK

From time to time I had received requests from numerous singers to coach them. After years of performing on every important stage in the country, and in every media, I had much knowledge and experience to impart to others. It was time to "give back." I knew I could be a great teacher, as I recalled the time when my brothers and I were in Basic Training during World War II at Camp Claiborne in Louisiana. One of our officers had asked me if I could form a chorus to sing at special Army functions. I thought, "Wow, what a great challenge!"

I remembered my father boasting to others that he could make the wall sing. I thought, "If he could do it, so can I." So I accepted the "challenge". Little did I realize that most of the GIs I was serving with, came from the hills, from farmlands in the South, and from Tennessee and Kentucky.

When the word got out, two hundred soldiers showed up at our battalion. I never expected that so many GIs would be interested in singing. But I guess they were as bored as I was. Anyway, I started with songs everyone knew like, "I've Been Working On The Railroad" and "Home On The Range." We sang in "unison" which meant without harmony. That would come later, after they gained the confidence that they could really sing. I was amazed at how powerful two hundred male voices could sound. After some sessions, I went to two-part harmony, with basses and tenors in separate sections. They shone with their newfound challenge. When the time came to do a show for the officers and camp personnel, we received standing ovations for our effort. I could not believe how fabulous they sounded and how wonderful they looked in their uniforms on our specially-built stage.

Songs like "Pack Up Your Troubles In Your Old Kit Bag" and other Army songs really got to everybody. Personally, I was astounded with my own ability to accomplish what I did. I guess I succeeded because I had given it my all.

One of the higher ranking officers, a Major, sent for me the next day. I couldn't understand why I was requested. He greeted me with a great big smile and complimented me on our performance. Then he sat me down and said, "We need people like you. How would you like me to recommend you for special training to become a Warrant Officer?" I was shocked! That sounded so good to me, to be appreciated for all my effort. After all, I was only a rookie.

I smiled and said, "Let me think about it. You know sir, that my brothers and I have been doing professional shows in camp, even though we're in different companies." I didn't think about it then, but I realized later that he was trying to separate the three of us, so I could end up alone with my company. Each company had a different destination overseas, and the Major needed me to provide recreational shows for our GIs.

It was a decision I had to discuss with Murray and Phil. When I told them I could become an officer, both of them said, "Are you crazy? You want to bust up our trio? You can't be serious!" I felt so guilty for even thinking about it.

I made an appointment with the Major and explained my predicament. I could tell he was disappointed by the glum look on his face. Then he said, "You know that eventually, you will be separated anyway." Little did he know that once again, as before in our lives, fate would intervene. We would soon be transferred into a "Special Service" company, to entertain the troops as a trio, till the war ended.

I had enjoyed teaching in the army so much, with guys who thought they couldn't sing, that I thought I would try it again. So I announced in Chicago newspapers that I would begin auditioning students for special vocal instruction. Singers flocked in. Most of them had stars in their eyes!

And why not? The future was wide open to them. They were young, eager, and ambitious. Just the prospect of maybe making it some day as performers, brought them hope and enthusiasm. Unfortunately, I had to make agonizing decisions at times. When 13-year-olds came with their parents to audition, I had to say "No" to many. Most of these young kids had been performing in their school plays and choruses. When their parents, relatives, and friends gave them standing ovations every time they sang, some were lulled into thinking they could make it big on Broadway.

Adults who knew me, felt that if I could coach them on the "ins and outs" of entertaining, they could go on to great careers as professionals. Perhaps so, but that was easier said than done. Some of my students were such fast learners, with good voices and personalities to match, that they were able to get "breaks" on their own. They were the aggressive ones, and an extreme pleasure for me to coach on the finer points of performing.

When Northwestern University music students needed extra money, they called to audition for my High Holiday Choir. Some of them had such glorious voices that the least I could do was to hire them. I went way over my budget, but I didn't have the heart to send them away. I just loaded my choir with extra singers who constantly stunned our congregants.

I was delighted to spend extra time with my star pupils. Some of them were strictly opera bound, while others just wanted to entertain. Now, years later, I'm thrilled to read about them, and to hear from protégés like Barbara Gray Nystrom, who has starred in the Phantom of the Opera, 42nd Street, and in opera companies overseas. When Gray sang in my choir, she needed to build her confidence. I kept assuring her that she could do what she thought she couldn't. It was sheer pleasure when I showed her how to hit the high C's. As Carlotta in "Phantom," she hits a high E—quite an accomplishment!

Others who studied with me entertained in my shows. One such performer was Shirlee Todd, who now sings and leads her own Band in songs that cater to different ethnic groups. Now I smile and am in a way rather embarrassed, that I never assigned a solo to Nancy Gustafson. She went on to star with the San Francisco Opera Company, and now is acclaimed as an outstanding soprano diva around the world. Then there was Salena, a prime coloratura soprano who appeared with me at Orchestra Hall. When she hit her high F at the end of *"Caro Nome,"* from the opera "Rigoletto," the house came down. Whatever she is doing now, she has my thanks for another wonderful memory. Finally, there is Ed Warble, my Scandinavian friend and protégé who is a super entertainer, and to whom I taught so many of my Jewish hits. He, too, has appeared with me in concert, and always refers to me as his special mentor and friend, which fills me with happiness and pride.

When I think of all the people I've had the privilege of helping, it gives me great satisfaction. But isn't that what life is all about—to be able to give back, again and again? Absolutely!

Chapter 52

THOUGHTS & OBSERVATIONS

Since returning to my roots as a cantorial messenger of my people, I have made it a daily ritual to pray for the needy, the sick, the poor and oppressed, and for world peace. Lately, I have been asking God to erase from my mind the darker moments I have experienced, especially during World War II. Although I didn't serve in the European theater, I am still devastated with the memory of our martyred brothers and sisters in the Holocaust! I also want to be able to forget the torn and ravaged bodies that I saw on Leyte's beaches in the Philippines. It pains me to remember how dead Japanese bodies were hacked in two. It pains me to remember how the Lind Brothers entertained the many severely wounded in hospitals, even though it was a *mitzvah*, a good deed, to do so. It pains me to remember seeing our G.I.s with no arms or legs and half their faces shot off. It pains me to remember how when we landed at Yokohama, the defeated Japanese kept bowing all the way down to the ground. Yes, we entered their homeland in triumph, but no one, even in defeat, should have to bow to another human being as his master. How pitiful to see them grovel in humiliation and shame. I'm certain there were many Japanese who abhorred the war as much as we did.

It was shocking for me to see three out of four buildings in Yokohama and Tokyo in rubble—with stones like monuments in a cemetery. I can only imagine the horror of seeing the charred bodies of tens of thousands of civilians in Hiroshima and Nagasaki, from the atomic bombs we dropped on them. Yes, it stopped the war, and probably saved an estimated 100,000 American lives, but it is nevertheless a terrible memory to live with for the rest of our lives. Whoever said "war is hell," had it so right.

My question to the world is: Do you think the day will ever come, when men of great intelligence and courage will sit together at a giant peace table, with leaders of every nation and race, under a new banner—declaring forevermore, Peace on Earth? Wasn't that what the United Nations was supposed to do? Will the politics of war ever cease, so we can create a better and safer world?

I believe that our bodies should be held sacred, as they were meant to be, not tortured or mangled or shot up by canon. I also believe strongly that our bodies house the spirit of God, and were meant for a much higher and more noble purpose. God is *One*, over all of us. It is therefore incumbent upon us to embrace all of humanity in a unity of faith! Can you imagine what a civilization without war would be like? That would truly be the greatest legacy we could ever leave to our children—no more wars! No more Holocausts! That is something worth dreaming about.

The father of our country, George Washington, bore his purpose proudly as he tried to bring justice to all Americans; Abraham Lincoln distinguished his presidency with his long fight for freedom from slavery and racial prejudice. The Pledge of Allegiance proclaims at its end, "With liberty and justice for all." I believe that now is the time to take each other by the hand and work together to beautify and rekindle the earth God gave us. I wonder what has changed us so that we disregard so many of the ethics of our fathers.

Is there nothing sacred any more? Is the getting and begetting of material things the only culture worth having, no matter how we achieve it?

Is compassion and mercy dead?

Is it better to rot in the poison of war or labor for the cause of peace?

Shall we let our universe suffocate in pollution, or should we shake off our lethargy and purify God's world?

Should we not fear the Tower of Babel in higher space that might come tumbling down, as we explore the mysteries of other planets while our own needs repair?

Such questions that torment my mind constantly make me long even more for the life I knew as a youngster. We had ambitions and hopes and our elders encouraged them. They gave us love and we admired their wisdom and accepted their discipline. Now God help us, the world grows smaller as terrorists are trying to blow up the world. The only vision I can endure is the light of hope that I see in the eyes of our children. Too many Americans are in a quagmire of confusion, as they "follow the leader." Where are the peacemakers? Where are the diplomats?

We seem to have no other choice but to look to our young for salvation. It is they, now, who will have to save our universe. It is they who will have to unpollute the polluted. It is they who must succeed where we have failed so miserably. Hopefully, it will be our children who will bring a greater sense of order, justice, and true peace to our world. The responsibility now falls on their shoulders to accomplish what we could not.

My dear father used to say, "The wheel of life turns constantly, and some day it will all return as it was, to a simpler and more meaningful existence." I wonder in that context, whether life as we knew it, will ever return. I turn my mind daily to the good things I've been lucky to be a part of, and I thank God for those glorious moments.

As I look back at my own life, I realize more and more, that being a celebrity of a kind, opened many doors I would never have dreamed possible. We were invited into the inner sanctums of the powerful as well as the oppressed. I observed so much and learned what made people tick, and how they looked at life. I learned about human nature and real values—what counts and what doesn't. Along with my brothers in our early years, we performed for people of every ilk and for audiences of every faith and creed.

We were fortunate to have sung with the greatest bands of our era. How can I possibly forget being accompanied by the Lou Breese Orchestra at the Chicago Theatre, the Milton De Lugg Band at the Broadway Strand in New York, The Woody Herman Orchestra in Chicago, and the Tommy Tucker Band at Universal Pictures. How I miss those fabulous years.

I believe, too, that what we need in these perilous times is more humor, to offset the 9/11 tragedy and the wars our country has suffered. I just wish some of the old-time comedians of our day were still around to make us laugh more. The geniuses of comedy like Charles Chaplin, Jack Benny, W. C. Fields, Red Skelton, Sid Caesar, Buster Keaton, Martha Raye, Danny Thomas, Danny Kaye, Shecky Green, and so many others did not need to use four-letter words to produce laughs. Theirs was clean comedy for the ages, for families, and for our children as well. They were brilliant performers who brought us pleasure beyond measure.

Lately, I ponder over the loss of so many of my show business friends. More recently, Henny Youngman, Alan King and Rodney Dangerfield have left us to join the distinguished roster of stars I am proud to have known. The sheer joy and laughter that they evoked from our Applaudiences still ring in my ears. To all of them, I raise my glass, filled with their favorite beverage, in a special toast: "May you find eternal peace as you dwell in the House of the Lord, and in the Shadow of His Wings."

Chapter 53

MY IDEOLOGY

I have always believed that Great men never die! Their works speak for them—be they in music, science, art, writing, or creating a different cultural legacy for the world. I also believe that our souls live on, and return again and again in "life after life." As we learn from the Jewish *Kabbalah* (mystic writings), our souls migrate from one body to the next at some point after our demise, continuing on and on, until our Supreme Creator says, "Mission Completed."

When bad things happened, I used to think, "My God, there has to be more to life than this constant battle. It would be intolerable to think that in the end, after all our labors and struggles, there are only ashes left of our existence." I always abhorred the word "death." To me, it always sounded so final and so wrong. Inherently, I believe in the immortality of the human soul!

Emily Brontë wrote about the invincibility of man with these words:
" There is no room for Death
Nor atom that His might could render void.
Thou art Being and breath
And what Thou art may never be destroyed."

Her words always brought me some modicum of comfort.

The renowned Indian philosopher and poet Rabindranath Tagore said: "Death is not extinguishing the light; it is putting out the lamp because the dawn has come." The greatest men of the century believed in life after death; that man is immortal: Socrates, Plato, Goethe, Henry James, Robert Milliken, Thomas Edison, and hundreds more believed in the affirmation of life.

Edison believed that the soul was a special thing that leaves the body at death. Our *Kabbalah* confirms that as well. For thousands of years, our sages believed that there is something way down deep that is eternal about every human being. Such thoughts and writings have led me to believe that our works are not in vain, that our true existence is beyond both time and space, that our souls transcend the body and live on after death, in a higher sphere, and in a larger capacity—where in conjunction with our Creator, we continue the work that we began here—on earth.

As we delve into the spiritual and feel the ties of togetherness formed in our children and grandchildren, as well as those who are drawn to us in friendship, I can't help but feel that the whole human family is connected in some way: past, present, and future.

As I ponder over and over the events and experiences I encountered in my lifetime, it is my observation that "success" in life can only be measured by the degree of dedication and commitment we put into our chosen works. My own life has been a seesaw of challenges. I would like to be remembered as one who through my voice lifted the spirits of my audiences. I have been divinely blessed and privileged to have been able to bring smiles, tears, and some measure of comfort and solace through my chanting and performing. Who, pray tell, could possibly ask for a greater gift than that?!

There is no doubt in my mind that I was born to sing. I am grateful for having been chosen to lead thousands of my brethren in prayer for most of my life. I am also grateful that I was able to celebrate with them at happy times, as well as to bring consolation when they suffered adversities. The last thirty years of my life have been the most rewarding times of my career. I bask in those memories, and at times I feel so blessed that I have been able to serve in so many capacities.

Many times I am asked when I'm going to retire, and I answer, "To what?" I am not one for the rocking chair, or to sit on my duff and twiddle my thumbs. I have to feel useful every day of my life, and I intend to face more "Applaudiences" as long as I am able.

I feel that everything I have done was part of my particular contribution to life. I believe that whatever I am, was, or hope to be, was all preordained long before I was born. I think that if I were conceived again in the same condition, I could not change my destiny one iota; that my restless heart and mind would drive me to the same conclusion: to fulfill my singular purpose, as all humans must fulfill their own destinies.

Thus I raise my eyes upward, appealing to the Father of all to lessen our frustrations and to grant us the inner and outer peace for which we yearn. Let the humor and joy of God and his angels prevail ever stronger in our hearts, so we can mock our adversities and bear with wisdom and laughter our common fate.

More than ever, I can now appreciate and echo the *krechtzing* (complaining) words of my sweet father Joshua. Through the years he constantly posed the eternal question as he stretched his arms upward to the heavens, crying out from the depths of his soul, *"Admosai, Gotteniu!"* "Why, oh God? And why me?" And to that I, too, add—*OY!*

Chapter 54

Epilogue

Having spent forty years of my life in the theatre, from the 30s to the 70s, in every theatrical medium from Broadway to Las Vegas, I can now look forward to a new era of performing Linds. My heart is glad that our grandchildren, Joanna and Allison, are now pursuing their own goals in theatre, following in the footsteps of the Lind Brothers, and my many years as a single performer. To me, life was all theatre, no matter what career I followed.

Therefore, it pleases me no end that I can now foresee a new generation of singing Linds, who will also be involved in theatre and face their own Applaudiences. This I know: hearing their familiar voices through the past and future, wherever I am, will lift my spirits and fulfill my hopes for a continuing legacy for years to come.

> I faced the challenges hurled at me
> Enduring for my art
> I stood up to adversity
> With courage in my heart.
>
> I came out singing, full of cheer
> And bared my woes to none,
> My purpose and my fate fulfilled
> A quite exciting run!

Applaudience: The Autobiography of Dale Lind

The Lind Family, 2007. Left to right back row: Allison, Sandra, Cary, Joanna. Front row: Jessie, Dale, Barbara

ABOUT THE AUTHOR

Born in Brooklyn, New York, to Jewish immigrant parents, Dale was tutored from the age of five by his father, famed Cantor Joshua Lind. At age nine, Dale was hailed as "the world's youngest cantorial prodigy." Emerging from tenement living, Dale and his brothers, Murray and Phil, formed their singing trio in 1938. In an era when radio, vaudeville, and night clubs were the main venues of entertainment, "The Three Lind Brothers" starred in them all, including guest appearances on Sid Caesar's "Show of Shows" and "The Rudy Valley Show."

As a GI in World War II, Dale witnessed the horrors of war in the South Pacific, the invasion of the Philippines, the return of General MacArthur to Leyte Island, and the signing of the Peace Treaty in Japan.

Entertaining thousands of troops with Danny Kaye, Danny Thomas, and other superstars, Dale and his brothers won the fame that catapulted them into headlines after the war. They performed in the most prestigious theaters and clubs in the US and Canada, and made a movie "short" for Universal Pictures.

In the late 1960s, Dale returned to Chicago as a solo performer and Cantor, eventually opening his own showplace, "The Pavillon." His performances and recordings thrilled thousands of followers, who labeled him, "Born to Sing."

ISBN 142516626-1